Changing
with
Lean Six Sigma

A. Aruleswaran

Published by LSS Academy Sdn. Bhd.
Edited by Thaatchaayini Kananatu
Cover Design & Illustrations by El Elyon Creations (001848341-V)
Printed by Akitiara Corporation Sdn. Bhd. (390199-U)

ISBN NO 978-983-44582-0-1

LSS Academy Sdn. Bhd. (797980-P)
No 4-2, Jalan Puteri 2/2, Bandar Puteri,
47100 Puchong, Selangor, Malaysia.
Tel : +603.8061.9055
Fax : +603.8061.4634
Check out our website at www.lss-academy.com

Table of Contents

Dedication

To the deeply missed Mr. S. Aruleswaran and Mr. K. Kananatu.

To my pillars of strength Thaatch and Vigna.

To my mother and mother-in-law, my brother, Ratni and brother-in-law, Kana and my sister, Roobini and sisters-in-law, Roobi (and Shukra) and Kalai (and Haymanth) who persevered during our recent emotional journey.

To my mentors Rich and Mr. Rama. Thank you.

Acknowledgements

Australasia: David Seacy, James Hildebrand, V. S. Pandian, CC Tham, Sabee Chai, Keith Gauntlett, Kenneth Chan, Sherman Yap, Helen Karuman, P. Deivindran, Lisa Custer, Aled Roberts.

Europe: Sabine von Hanstein, Sibylle Mutschler, Stephan Lunau, Matthew Gracie, Tom Farley.

North America: Rich Hirsh, Mark Gallerneault, Andrew Hobbis, Keith Waterson, Robert Naud, Kevin Gatenby, John Woehlke, Helene Legace, Michael Arendt, Joe Wright, Som Das, Mark McMulan, Cam Laing.

A Preface to
Changing with Lean Six Sigma

There are many books written about Lean, Six Sigma, Lean Sigma and Lean Six Sigma. For most parts these books describe the origins of the tools and elaborate on the techniques that are successfully used to execute projects.

I wrote this book because of my interest in this subject, both as a practitioner and consultant. This book is centered on **change management** that is required in an organization that intends to improve using Lean Six Sigma. It builds on the literature that I have read, in particular *Lean Six Sigma* by Michael George, and the numerous challenges that I have experienced whilst deploying Lean Six Sigma initiatives. The most significant challenge is to change people and their mindsets.

The heart of this book is to introduce to you that **Change** is an essential factor for success and that Lean Six Sigma is a proven organizational toolset that can bring about and implement Change.

This book also builds on the successes that Asian based organizations have achieved with Lean Six Sigma. The intention is to encourage even more organizations to follow suit.

I hope with the examples presented in this book, organization wide transformation with Lean Six Sigma will be embraced with confidence in order to introduce the necessary **change** that can lead to a new level of business excellence and performance.

The book is divided into three sections. Section one introduces the subject and the factors to be considered to establish a Lean Six Sigma Organization. Section two discusses the philosophy of change and the role of Lean Six Sigma in establishing organization wide change. Section three looks at Lean Six Sigma applications in Asian organizations that have successfully changed with Lean Six Sigma.

A. Aruleswaran
14 April 2009

Foreword

Able Leadership

– V.S. Pandian, FranklinCovey Malaysia

I am pleased to write this Foreword to Dr. Arul's book on Lean Six Sigma.

2009 will prove a challenge for individuals and organizations as a result of the collapse of the world financial system. Wealth will erode for individuals, families, enterprises and nations. Those that are able to survive and thrive are going to be watched and admired. Stories will invariably be written on how they were able to come through in one piece, and in some cases, to even do better in this year of gloom and doom.

For the many amongst us who are anxious about implementing a success strategy that will work during this difficult moment, this book by Dr. Arul offers some concrete measures to get started in the right direction.

Lean Six Sigma (LSS) involves working on both the top line (revenue) as well as the bottom-line (profits) of the enterprise. The attention to the top line is by being relevant to customer needs (Voice of the Customer), and the attention to the bottom-line is through better quality, improved cycle times and lower costs.

I'll venture to suggest that contrary to the popular action to reducing headcount to reduce operational costs, enterprises should instead enhance their business operations through reduction of waste, better quality and improved processes. It is useful to remember that human capital is a great asset that will pay handsome dividends during good times and bad. It's a question of how leaders inspire and bring out the best in them.

To support the successful implementation of LSS initiatives, an enterprise needs the correct blend of able leadership and competent management.

Able leadership involves 4 core competencies that a leader at every level of the enterprise should possess in order to effectively lead his or her team to execute the organization's important goals:

1. The ability to inspire trust and confidence in the followers, to give hope;

2. The ability to chart a strategic direction for the team and the organization so that the followers can see the 'big picture' clearly and are motivated to give their best;

3. The ability to develop operational excellence through best-in-class work processes, systems, procedures and policies—this is where LSS initiatives fit; and

4. The ability to unleash the talent and potential of the people.

These core competencies are leadership imperatives to lead today's knowledge worker.

Competent management is required in order to ensure that LSS project selection and execution is of the highest standard, for otherwise, valuable talent and other resources may not be put to optimal use.

In our work with client organizations for the past 16 years, we have found that our FranklinCovey curriculum offerings provide some of the best principle-based leadership and management solutions to ensure successful LSS implementation.

To begin your own LSS journey, this book will serve as a good source of information. Dr. Arul is an LSS practitioner of international stature. This book draws from his practical insights on the subject.

It is never too late to prepare your enterprise to be 'lean and mean'!

Best wishes.

V.S. Pandian
CEO
FranklinCovey Malaysia
www.franklincoveymalaysia.com
February 2009

Foreword

Business Improvement Through Structured Problem Solving

– Rich Hirsh, Novelis Inc. USA

Ready, aim, fire; the sequence sounds completely logical and natural as we repeat it. From our conceptual understanding of this process, to the actuation of the steps, something intervenes to alter the process to ready, fire, aim. The driver for many is the pressure, real or perceived, to deliver fast results, and the allure of being the one to receive the accolades for solving the problem. This need for the quick fix becomes our culture and our adrenaline addiction.

So it goes for many organizations which focus on addressing the symptoms and the quick fix, moving from issue to issue, never realizing their solutions propagate their inventory of future problems; a somewhat self-fulfilling prophecy. Many have neither the perceived time to stop chasing their tail, or the methods to reach root-cause driven countermeasures.

The methods to be described in this book offer insight into a powerful alternative approach. Not a series of quick fixes to a variety of symptoms, but rather an investment in developing the problem solving capacity of the organization through the use of structured problem solving methodologies. I said investment since what is needed is a journey both individually and as a collective organization.

As you have chosen to read a book on improvement, it's clear you've taken the first step, self-commitment to learning. As many individuals from your business do the same, you collectively begin to realize there is a better way to stop the endless cycle of symptomatic solutions. The fundamental process you are beginning involves learning, then learning reinforcement by doing.

All problems begin in the same way as small issues left unattended. These procrastinated issues cling together and form mid-size and larger problems. This typical apathetic approach of dealing with problems creates the practice of daily firefighting when those issues exceed our pain threshold. Once these issues reach a mid or large size, a much larger set of powerful tools is required; hence the use of Lean Six Sigma (LSS) to break down problems into their components and focus on the 20% of the inputs causing 80% of the variation in the desired result.

The fundamental approach with LSS is to reduce variation in the desired output metric by identifying and controlling the critical input variables. Once this process variation is reduced, and the processes capability to meet Customer requirements is improved, opportunities for quality, cost, delivery, and growth are created. Although this sounds quite easy, the toolset required must be deep, statistically sound, and rigorously executed. The essential change is to move from emotional decisions making to a data driven basis.

Within this book you'll be introduced to the fundamentals of LSS so that you can begin your journey. My advice is to pay close attention to the very useful case study on Sustaining a Deployment and the Multi-Generational Plan approach. You will find this a great technique to lay out a multi-tiered plan to identifying the right set of projects to undertake to reach a timed set of objectives. Proper planning makes for perfect performance!

As this book comes to press in 2009, most of the world is suffering through one of the worst economic recessions seen in the last 75 years. Companies around the world slash fixed asset costs until they have little left to rationalize except their revenue streams. Eventually even these are considered. All the time, the waste around them goes unnoticed; it's become ingrained in the operation. The necessity of survival is the perfect backdrop to challenge the organization for the improvements desperately needed creating the burning platform to rally upon.

Lean Six Sigma is a proven way to deliver those needed results. Results focused on achieving the annual plans of the business and growing the organization. Closing the gaps we don't know how to achieve. Sustaining those gains; to continue producing the results desired. Developing employees to learn to see, overcome problems, and deal with the reality of the changing marketplace and Customer requirements.

Best of luck to you on your journey toward improvement!

Rich Hirsh
Global Continuous Improvement Director,
Master Black Belt
Novelis, Inc. Cleveland, Ohio, USA
Rich.hirsh@novelis.com

Section ONE

A Lean Six Sigma Organization

Chapter 1

Introducing Lean Six Sigma To Your Organization

A step in the right direction

Businesses over the last decade have tried, tested or adopted Six Sigma for one specific reason: the savings generated by Six Sigma impacts the bottom line.

Successful organizations like GE, Caterpillar and Alcan have utilized Six Sigma to narrow the gap between shareholders' expectations and results. They have made Six Sigma the tool and methodology of continuous improvement. Six Sigma starts with a vision, followed by strategy development and ends with execution.

The alignment and unification of strategy and execution to deliver results has successfully led to the development and empowerment of human capital, bringing it towards high performance of continuous improvement in the entire Six Sigma organization[1].

The GE, Caterpillar and Alcan experiences have made Six Sigma the favourite methodology of business leaders today. It provides the unifying language and foundation that establishes business goals and brings cultural empowerment. This creates focus towards maximizing value to the business and shareholders.

FOCUS

Figure 1.1 : Strategy Meets Execution[2]

What is Lean?

Lean was introduced as a production methodology that focuses on a business' internal need to maximize value added activities (which customers would pay for) and the reduction of waste that increases the cost of running a business. It was popularized by the Toyota Production Systems.

Lean focuses on:

1. Increasing process speed through the elimination of complexities;

2. Utilizing tools that analyze process flows, constraints and time delays at each step of the process; and

3. Identifying value added and value enabling activities through the elimination of non-value added activities known as waste.

The modern Lean production additionally focuses on improving process flow by addressing the imbalance (in resources or materials) and creating a production level that acts as a "pull process".

What is Six Sigma?

Six Sigma usually finds its way into an organization as a quality improvement method due to its reputation of using statistical tools to measure quality and precision of a product or service.

Since its conception in the early eighties, Six Sigma has evolved from a mere statistical quality improvement technique into an established methodology that provides businesses with a comprehensive toolset to improve the capability of business processes and quality of products and services.

Six Sigma emphasizes on the need for improvement in business performance that leads to minimizing defects, for example, not meeting a customer's specification or specific service requirement. In addition, Six Sigma also addresses variation in process and in quality that deters the capability of consistently producing high quality products and services.

The terminologies that are synonymous to Six Sigma include:-

1. The DMAIC Cycle (Define –Measure –Analyse –Improve –Control) – a problem solving roadmap (see Figure 1.2);

2. The measure of DPMO (Defects Per Million Opportunity) as Six Sigma quality – a measure of process performance and quality based on non–conformance to a quality specification; and

3. The VOC (Voice of Customer) – a method utilized to determine a customer's wants and needs that is organized and structured with key measures and metrics to establish and evaluate quality standards.

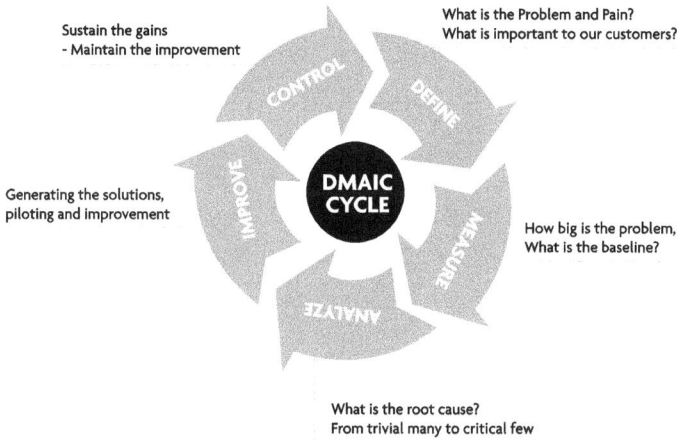

Figure 1.2 : The DMAIC Cycle

What is Lean Six Sigma?[1]

The Lean and Six Sigma combination is the new Six Sigma generation. This new methodology is the offspring of two very essential components of business process improvement that complement and reinforce one another.

Lean aims to create value through the elimination of waste and non value-added activities. Six Sigma on the other hand, is the measure of quality and meeting the customer's needs. Lean on its own cannot bring a process under statistical control to achieve quality targets, whilst Six Sigma alone cannot significantly improve process speed or reduce waste that can improve operational cost and capital.

Separately they enable two characteristic voices that are critical for business success:

1. The **Voice of the Customer** which facilitates the characteristic and measure of quality through Six Sigma; and

2. The **Voice of the Business** that permits the characteristic of speed through Lean processes and operations.

In the combination of Lean Six Sigma, a third fusion voice, which is often overlooked is the **Voice of the Employee** (VOE). VOE represents people investment and human capital empowerment.

As many businesses would have experienced and are continuing to experience, subscribing to a process improvement solution or system alone is not sufficient to unify strategy and execution, if the culture of the organization fails to engage its people to use, adopt and adapt that solution or system.[3] The empowerment of human capital becomes the cornerstone of establishing a continuous improvement culture and this requires the fusion of Lean and Six Sigma.

Lean Six Sigma is a methodology driven by the need to change, to continuously improve and eliminate complexities, and to meet the goals of the business and shareholders though a single crucial element – the Voice of the Employee, or simply put, organizational effectiveness.

Quality

**Six Sigma
Focus**

**Lean
Focus**

Costs

**Shorter
Delivery
Times**

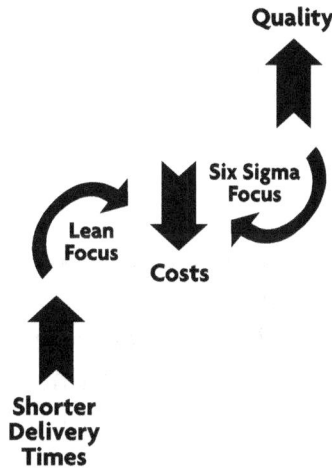

Figure 1.3 : Lean Six Sigma Strategy[2]

A Continuous Improvement Culture

The foundation of a continuous improvement culture begins with a focus on results. When an organization embarks on such an initiative, trailing the path of successful business leaders like Jack Welch and Warren Buffet, they integrate Vision, Strategy and Execution into the essence of the organization's culture. Despite this, many organizations at their own peril disconnect the business and customer strategy from the foundation of their continuous improvement activity.

The key to a successful continuous improvement culture is the management of infrastructure that effectively translates strategic agendas into continuous improvement initiatives. These initiatives are aimed at maximizing value and results that are directly linked to profit and loss that can be effectively tracked and managed.

Lean Six Sigma should not be adopted to replace an existing methodology or management system but the best aspects of both can be integrated to create a sustainable continuous improvement culture.

What's in it for your organization?

A business organization exists fundamentally to earn profits. Its shareholders, stakeholders, directors and managers aim to achieve vital business goals *inter alia* results, revenue, growth and Return Of Invested Capital (ROIC).

The key question is: How can a methodology or a quality and speed improvement toolset like Lean Six Sigma help your organization achieve these goals? What's in it for your organization?

When management begins to understand that Lean Six Sigma unifies strategy and execution, this becomes vital in achieving their corporate goals. As Lean Six Sigma is intergrated into management thought and practice, leadership engagement can be achieved.

Leadership engagement instills the culture of continuous improvement. The framework of *Define, Measure, Analyze, Improve* and *Control* (DMAIC) together with information such as data, customers, quality, speed and processes become a norm in the organization.

Through human capital empowerment, characteristic voices like the Voice of Customer, the Voice of Business and the Voice of Employee are successfully enabled to ensure products and services offered to customers translate to goals and results that ultimately maximize the ROIC. This fulfills the fundamental purpose of your organization, which is to earn profits!

What's in it for you?

Can we effectively and consistently eliminate the problems that form the daily and routine issues that affect our job performance?

The DMAIC methodology brings a rigour to the Lean Six Sigma organization. It provides the organization with a roadmap on how to resolve problems that affect quality and productivity. The methodology encourages empowerment and furnishes everyone with a vast array of toolsets. Through this, everyone is able to generate results that would be consistent in terms of output. Thus, the organization will have a consistent method of addressing the Voice of the Customer, Voice of the Business and Voice of the Employee, the elements that drive business results. This makes Lean Six Sigma an enabler that drives a continuous improvement culture.

Every employee in an organization becomes a driver of results. Organizations that adopt Lean Six Sigma will have company wide drivers of results aligned to its vision and strategy.

What's in it for you? With Lean Six Sigma and the DMAIC framework and tools you become the DNA of your organization and the future leader that aligns employee mindset to business strategy and customer needs.

As Anne Mulcahy, CEO and Chairman of Xerox Corporation noted:

"Lean Six Sigma is not tools...it's the infrastructure and discipline in place to make business improvement an imperative. It will be painful, we will select and train our best people, those we can least afford to reassign, our future leaders, to enable a cultural change."

Becoming A Lean Six Sigma Organization

"Its all about finding best practices, adapting them, and continually improving them. When you do that right, new product and service ideas, new processes, and opportunities for growth start to pop out everywhere and actually become the norm." This is exactly what happened at GE under Jack Welch's leadership.

Lean Six Sigma is a methodology that is proven. It is focused, disciplined and simple. It is a journey, starting with a step in the right direction.

Endnotes:
1. *Michael L George, Lean Six Sigma, McGraw-Hill, 2002 and Michael George et al, What is Lean Six Sigma, McGraw-Hill, 2003.*
2. *George Group Consulting, Alcan – George Group Lean Six Sigma Course Notes, Nov 2003.*
3. *David Seacy, Kirtland Leadership, Australia, Discussions Notes – Alcan Green Belt Training, Malaysia Nov 2003.*

Chapter 2

Lean Six Sigma and the DMAIC Methodology

Enabling business performance

Speed, customer satisfaction and low costs through operational excellence are essential goals for businesses that offer products and services to customers. However, a business' ultimate goal is to achieve and sustain superior shareholder returns.

Organizations in the manufacturing, banking, insurance, retail and government sectors usually drive towards prioritising operational excellence because the bulk of their costs are operations cost. Analysis by Lean and Six Sigma consultants show that 30% to 80% of the costs in a service business are pure waste. Eliminating this waste can not only reduce costs, but more importantly allow businesses and services to become faster and more responsive to customers, ultimately driving revenue growth.

Applying Lean Six Sigma

Lean Six Sigma is a **data driven** principle and process optimization toolset adopted by businesses to enhance process or service efficiency, customer satisfaction, eliminate waste and reduce operational costs.

The traditional perception of industries is that a **gain** in excellence for a particular key performance area requires a **trade off** in excellence in other significant key performance areas. An example of this traditional paradigm is shown in Figure 2.1.

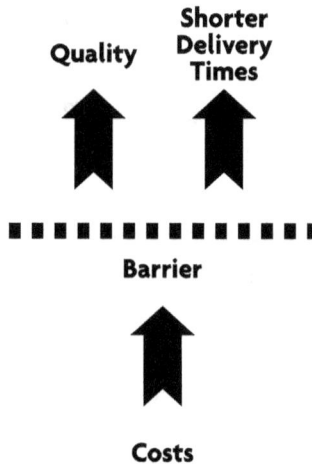

Figure 2.1 : Traditional Improvement Paradigm[1]

Lean Six Sigma challenges this traditional perception. The Lean Six Sigma paradigm states that a **gain** in excellence in a key performance area can be achieved with a **gain** in excellence in all significant key performance areas, as illustrated in Figure 2.2.

**Shorter
Delivery
Times**

Quality   **Costs**

No Barrier

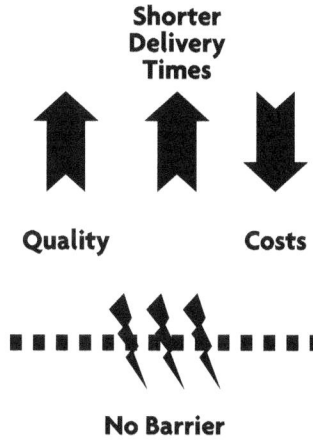

Figure 2.2 : Lean Six Sigma Paradigm[1]

To integrate a Lean Six Sigma paradigm into the organization, a methodology is required. This is provided by the DMAIC methodology. DMAIC gives focus in deployment and implementation of continuous improvement activities in the operational routine, ensures flawless execution and produces rapid results. Not only that, the success of Lean Six Sigma lies in the rigorous adoption of the DMAIC methodology.

The DMAIC Methodology

The DMAIC methodology is:
Define – Measure – Analyse – Improve – Control.

It is a method to solve problems that affect business performances that are identified through the fundamental voices: Voice of Customer, Voice of Business and Voice of Employee. These problems at the outset have unknown solutions, hence solving them becomes a critical business need. The need to continuously improve makes DMAIC the overriding methodology to establish a problem-solving framework.

DMAIC allows a business to first identify a practical problem **(Define)**, secondly to convert it to a statistical problem **(Measure)**, then to generate and pilot a statistical solution **(Analyse & Improve)** and finally to apply a practical solution **(Control)**.

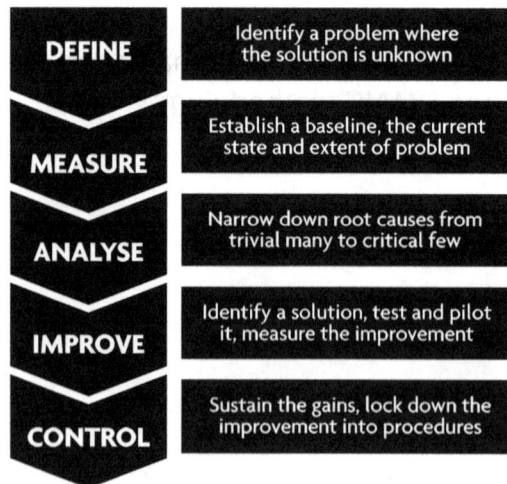

DEFINE	Identify a problem where the solution is unknown
MEASURE	Establish a baseline, the current state and extent of problem
ANALYSE	Narrow down root causes from trivial many to critical few
IMPROVE	Identify a solution, test and pilot it, measure the improvement
CONTROL	Sustain the gains, lock down the improvement into procedures

Figure 2.3 : DMAIC Methodology

Define

In the **Define** phase, a problem or an improvement opportunity, with no known solution, is identified and scoped. A problem statement is developed to describe the business "pain" that requires solving or the improvement that is needed. Factors that are critical to customer's quality requirements are identified. The problem is defined in terms of measurable criteria or metrics. This is supported by the extent and consequences of not solving the problem.

Measure

In this phase, a baseline data for the problem is first established. The ability to accurately measure the Critical To customer's Quality (CTQ) and the metrics is determined. The process in which the problem is occurring or where the improvement is required is mapped out in detail and this would include time, people and material elements to ensure that the state of the current value stream (Value Stream Map) is clearly understood.

Impact to the CTQ is established by identifying the key input and output variables of the problem. These measures are essential to verify the capability and stability of the process.

Analyse

The aim of this phase is to identify the root cause of the problem. In this phase, a thorough data analysis is carried out to filter the reasons of a problem from the "trivial many" to the "critical few". The relationship between the input and output variables will be established.

Additionally, activities such "cause and effect" study, "time and motion" analysis, analysis of statistical data and a "failure mode effects" analysis will be performed. The results of these are expected to assist with the validation of the "critical few" root-causes.

Improve

This is the most crucial phase where upon identifying the root-causes, solutions would be generated and tested by conducting a pilot. During this phase, team creativity often helps to generate solutions and reach a consensus that result in maximum gains. A draft future state value stream map, work instructions and standard operating procedures will be developed to facilitate the execution of the pilot.

Data collected from the pilot will then be compared against the baseline data (from the **Measure** phase) as an extent of improvement. Risk analysis can be carried out to determine the impact of stakeholders not accepting a solution.

Control

At the **Control** phase, the improvements identified during the **Improve** phase would be captured and thoroughly documented. All information would be gathered, consolidated and prioritised to aid a final or full scale implementation. Implementation plans as well as change management procedures will be developed to ensure a successful transition of the solution to the team that will ultimately be responsible to sustain the new and improved process.

A roadmap of how the problem was solved will then be established.

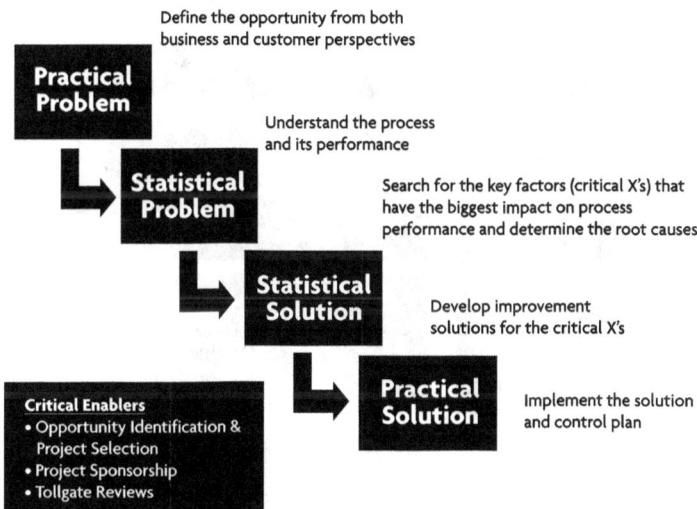

Define the opportunity from both business and customer perspectives

Practical Problem

Understand the process and its performance

Statistical Problem

Search for the key factors (critical X's) that have the biggest impact on process performance and determine the root causes

Statistical Solution

Develop improvement solutions for the critical X's

Critical Enablers
• Opportunity Identification & Project Selection
• Project Sponsorship
• Tollgate Reviews

Practical Solution

Implement the solution and control plan

Figure 2.4 : DMAIC Problem Solving Approach[1]

DMAIC Roadmap

With the DMAIC methodology a consistent and standardized manner of problem solving can be applied throughout the organization. The rigour of each DMAIC phase will assist to ensure a problem is solved or an improvement is achieved. The methodology itself becomes a roadmap that enables a transformation towards business performance.

DEFINE	• Project Charter • Voice of Customer & Business • High Level Process Map • Team Onboarding & Workplan • Sponsor Sign-off
MEASURE	• Baseline Data, Output Measures • Data Collection Plan • Key Input and Output Variables • Basic Statistical Analysis • Value Stream Mapping
ANALYSE	• Waste & Value Analysis • Time & Motion Analysis • Input Measures & Correlation • Regression & Variance Analysis • Cause & Effect – Root Cause
IMPROVE	• Gather, Consolidate & Prioritise • Creativity Techniques & FMEA • Optimization & Mistake Proofing • Piloting & Solution Tests • Implementation Plans & Measures
CONTROL	• Documentations & Instructions • Implementation & Handover Plans • Monitoring & Reaction Plan • Control & Validation Tools • Closure Report

Figure 2.5 : DMAIC Cheat Sheet[2]

Endnotes:

1. *George Group Consulting, Alcan–George Group Lean Six Sigma Course Notes, Nov 2003.*
2. *Rich Hirsh, Novelis Kingston Black Belt Training, Discussion Notes – Summer 2005.*
3. *Michael George et al, The Lean Six Sigma Pocket Toolbook: A Quick Reference Guide to 100 Tools for Improving Quality and Speed, McGraw–Hill, 2004.*

Notes on Lean Six Sigma Quality

The term Six Sigma is derived from the study of production statistics known as process capability studies. When Six Sigma was invented, Motorola referred to it as the ability of manufacturing processes to produce a very high proportion of output within customers' specification. Lean on the other hand ensured that waste in manufacturing processes is eliminated.

Today, processes that operate with a Lean Six Sigma Quality are assumed to create long-term defect levels that are below 3.4 defects per million opportunities (DPMO). This is equal to 99.9997% of quality. Lean Six Sigma's implicit goal is to improve all processes to a level of 3.4 DPMO quality or better[1].

Percent	DPMO
93%	66,800
98%	22,700
99%	6,210
99.87%	1,350
99.9997%	3.4

Figure 2.6 : Sigma Quality Level[1]

Is 99.9997% Good Enough?
– The "goodness level" of 99.9997% equates to:

Postal Services
losing 30,000 mails
per hour

Electric Utilities
Services failing for 10
hours monthly

Public Health Services
performing 3,000 incorrect
surgical procedures weekly

Water Utilities
producing daily 30
minutes of unsafe
drinking water

1 aborted take-off
or landing daily at
a major airport

Prescription of
100,000 wrong drugs
annually

Chapter 3

Changing into a Lean Six Sigma Organization

> "Six Sigma is better than a trip to the dentist."
> *– Jack Welch, former CEO of General Electric.*

The transition towards performance

"Can a program such as Six Sigma and Lean Production or Lean Six Sigma be incorporated into an organization? Can it enable us to achieve goals like revenue growth, economic profit and shareholder returns?"

"Can any of these programs that have shown great success in the world of manufacturing in companies like Motorola and Toyota, since the early 1980's and in the world of finance, service and transactions in companies such as GE Capital and Xerox since the mid 1990's, be made into a success in today's world of Information and Communication Technology (ICT)?"

Creating a continuous improvement culture

Dynamic business environments require an organization to develop the ability to adopt change and continuously improve. The inability to change exposes the organization to risks associated with failing to know and understand the Voice of Customer, the Voice of Business and the Voice of Employee.

To change, an organization requires a clearly defined and articulated "burning platform". The "burning platform" creates an internal drive to focus on results which becomes the foundation of a continuous improvement culture. Organizations that embark on change by identifying the "burning platform" and integrating it into its vision, strategy and execution, can then seek enterprise wide **leadership engagement.** This has been demonstrated by successful Lean Six Sigma organizations like GE Capital, Xerox and Alcan.

What is a "burning platform"?

It is a message for change and improvement from the leader of a business, e.g. CEOs, COOs. The leader articulates the need for change and shows why the organization must use the Lean Six Sigma principles to improve the organization. The message must contain specific goals to accomplish over a period of one to three years.

Changing a business into a performance oriented organization is a challenge and the transition for change requires perseverance. As management **envisions** its corporate goals, it will realize that a unified strategy and **execution** are vital prerequisites. The business then begins to **experience** its ability to meet objectives and critical business needs. Change is embraced by the whole organization, making the creation of a continuous improvement culture possible.

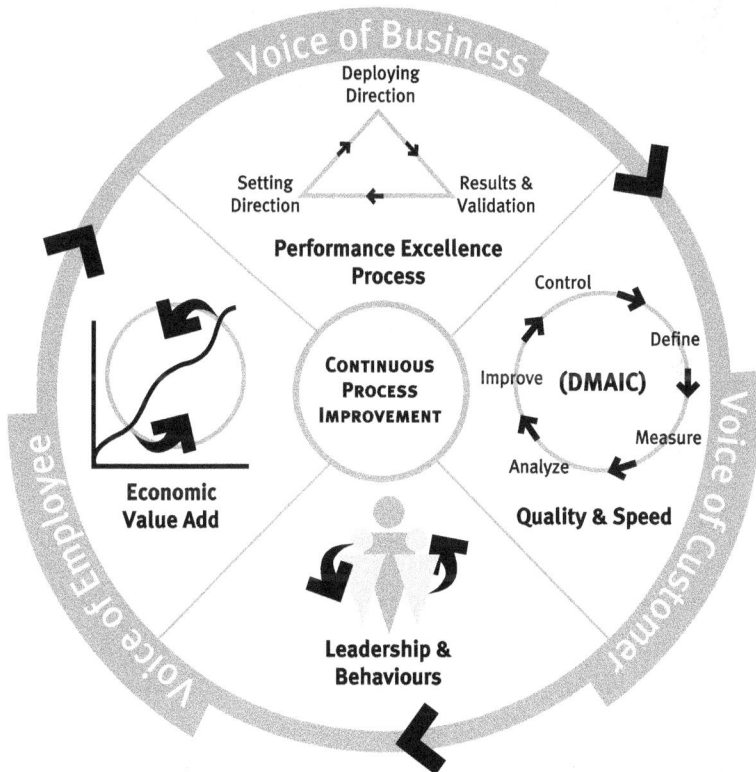

Figure 3.1 : Voice of Customer, Business & Employee

There are four change factors that have the biggest leverage in ensuring that change towards a continuous improvement culture is sustainable.

Change Factor One: Leadership Engagement

> "I've watched enough change programs
> and change efforts to know that
> the key is leadership."
> *– Lou Guiliano, CEO if ITT Industries)*

To ensure that initial continuous improvement efforts are translated to long term sustainable gains, management needs to instinctively understand that Lean Six Sigma is imperative. A momentum for Lean Six Sigma can be created by having management participate in decisions that affect the daily use of Lean Six Sigma. This can be maintained by integrating the DMAIC methodology into management thinking and practices.

"We need to put in some significant effort in the beginning to get this huge ball of a Continuous Improvement program rolling throughout the departments. The management's responsibility is to give it the inertia that will start the ball rolling. Once it hits the ground running at a constant speed, all we would need to do is to give it the constant taps to ensure that the momentum is maintained. This is leadership engagement and it is management's responsibility," says a Vice President of a corporation.

Change Factor Two:
Quick Starts and Hits

"Can we effectively and consistently harvest the low hanging fruits?"

Which fruit to pick?

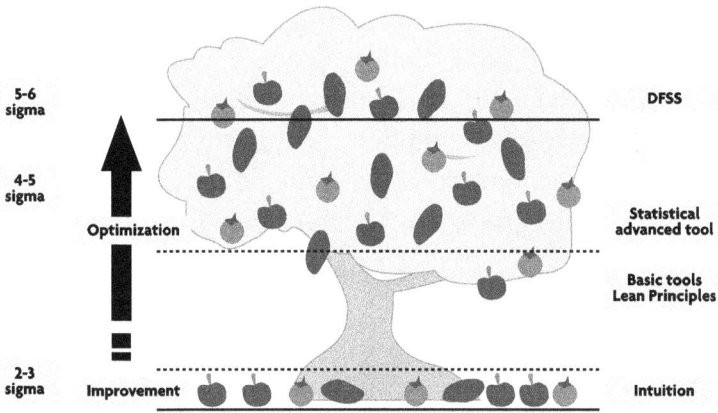

Figure 3.2 Sigma Quality Level and Quick Hits

Quick Starts and Hits are essential in order to aim and achieve crucial results. This means using the Lean Six Sigma toolset to identify continuous improvement activities that will achieve maximum benefit with the least effort (low hanging fruits). Quick Starts and Hits are vital to eliminate skepticism on continuous improvement initiatives and achieving fast results through Lean Six Sigma becomes a key to sustaining and maintaining a momentum of change.

> "It is common sense to take a method and try it. If it fails, admit it frankly and try another. But above all, try something."
> – *Franklin D. Roosevelt*

How to do this? Organizations should first look at training a corporate Lean Six Sigma deployment team. Then use Kaizen and Financial Value Trees to establish specific deployment targets and metrics. Next, rapidly execute initiatives that will achieve those identified targets. Quick Starts and Hits aims to show forward moving and positive progress that can gather further support for change.

What is Kaizen?

Kaizen is a Japanese term for continuous improvement where problem solving activities at a department or production facility is executed rapidly to achieve quick gains. It is a Lean tool made popular by the Toyota Production System.

Change Factor Three: Organizing for Success

Without the requisite change and alignment in people's mindsets, continuous improvement cannot be achieved. In order to embark on this, one needs to address the cultural and technical barriers, organize constructive team dynamics and engage leaders.

Ultimately change and transition begins with the establishment of a continuous improvement infrastructure with clearly defined roles and responsibilities and a reporting channel that can access the "C" level management. This would generate the discipline that makes continuous improvement a business imperative.

A continuous improvement infrastructure is the price that a business needs to pay to succeed in Lean Six Sigma.

At the helm of such an infrastructure is the Executive Leadership including the CEO and the top management, who are responsible in setting up the vision for a Lean Six Sigma deployment. They are followed by the Lean Six Sigma Champions, who are empowered with the independence and resources to identify the strategy for improvements and the responsibility to execute the implementation across the organization. Below them are the Change Agents.

Change Factor Four:
Value Creation

Value Creation is the ability to generate outputs that impact a business' financial performance. It refers broadly to the need to improve vital business parameters like Financial Performance, Operational Processes, the Voice of Customers and Products or Services in offer. An integral component of this is the use of a value-based project selection methodology which requires relevant and balanced resources towards continuous improvement efforts and strategic objectives.

Value Creation requires garnering of management commitment to improve products and services that are not meeting a customer's needs. Often this is done through delegation or simply put, "passing the buck". A value-based project selection methodology needs the management's efficiency in allocating resources which is usually expected from delegation. However, in a Lean Six Sigma program, the personal involvement of business leaders by championing and sponsoring initiatives will ensure its effectiveness.

The value-based project selection methodology is linked to strategic goals, revenue, profit and ROIC. This can only be effective with sponsors and champions of Lean Six Sigma. The value creation achieved here becomes the essence of institutionalizing a successful continuous improvement infrastructure.

Conclusion

"It's all about finding best practices, adapting them, and continually improving them. When you do that right, new product and service ideas, new processes, and opportunities for growth start to pop out everywhere and actually become the norm," says a Lean Six Sigma Executive Champion.

This is exactly what happened at GE under Jack Welch's leadership. Companies successfully adopting Lean Six Sigma continuously look at ways to keep it alive and evolving. New ways, tools and techniques are developed and integrated into the organization.

Results are always based on performance that would continuously outpace competitors and market indices. It is driven by all the four change factors and most importantly the first factor – leadership engagement. Engaged leaders aligned to achieve strategic goals can ensure that a continuous improvement program continues to survive and the change can be affected at the DNA level of the organization – its human capital.

Endnotes:
1. *Michael L George, Lean Six Sigma, McGraw-Hill, 2002.*
2. *Michael George et al, What is Lean Six Sigma, McGraw-Hill, 2003.*
3. *George Group Consulting, Alcan-George Group Lean Six Sigma Course Notes, Nov 2003.*
4. *Jack Welch, Winning, Collins Business, 2005.*

Notes on Lean Six Sigma Change Agents

A Lean Six Sigma organization creates and maintains a pool of Change Agents trained and equipped with Lean Six Sigma toolsets. They are commonly known as Black Belts, Green Belts and Yellow Belts depending on their level of training. Change Agents can develop to become Continuous Improvement Experts who are a part of a special Lean Six Sigma infrastructure created to drive goals to achieve changes within the organization.

Change Agents are the future leaders of an organization who are responsible for an effective achievement of business goals. Being a Change Agent in a Lean Six Sigma organization is not about being trained to execute Lean Six Sigma projects, it is about cultivating the ability to recognize and undertake the specific Lean Six Sigma projects that will not only realize business goals but also enable potential changes in the mindset of the entire organization.

Selecting the Change Agents for Lean Six Sigma is a challenge for any organization that has set its sights to ensuring that the business goals are to be met. It requires the management to release its best candidates, and most often the staff or colleagues who are successfully managing and executing the present status quo of process and product quality.

It forces them to understand that having Lean Six Sigma Black Belts and Green Belts for the sake of Lean Six Sigma alone will not give the organization the millions in savings that it aims for. Effectiveness of change will only take place if these Change Agents are enabled to reach their fullest potential.

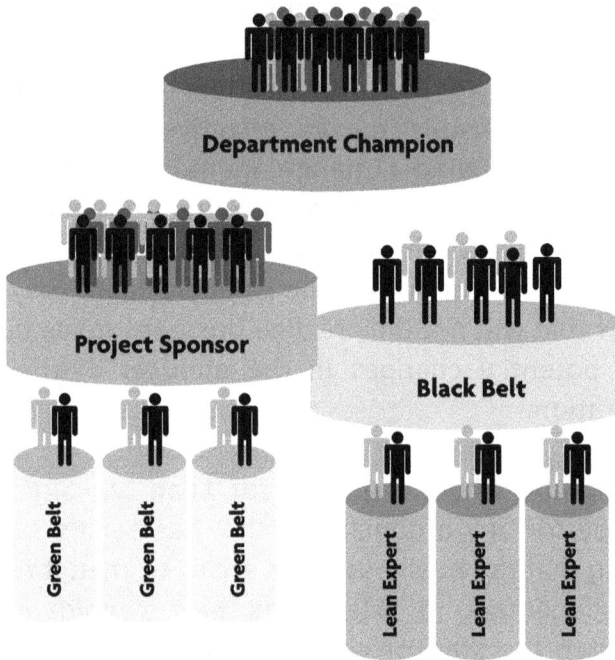

Figure 3.3 Lean Six Sigma Change Agents

Section TWO

Lean Six Sigma and Change

Chapter 4

Stepping Stones Towards Greatness

> "They must often change, who would be
> constant in Happiness or Wisdom."
> *– Confucius*

Change can establish a business, develop new products and services and inspire innovation. Ideally, change should be embedded into a business from its inception and developed as the business grows. Change can lead a business to greatness.

Many modern businesses today have taken the lead to change by adopting and adapting Lean Six Sigma, but it is by no means a "quick fix" to their problems. In order to strengthen your muscles, you have to first exercise them. In the same way, change once embedded within a business organization must be constantly exercised in order to strengthen its capacity.

But, is it easy to change? Do businesses have the capability to change? To flex the muscles of change it requires time, effort and a big dose of persistence. After all, success is 1% inspiration and 99% perspiration!

The status quo effect

A business can easily embrace change when it establishes itself but it is often unable to **exercise change** once a business momentum or status quo is established. The momentum or status quo once fixed – for example revenue, operating costs and profits (or loss) – the business is totally consumed by its focus to deliver to its customers. There is neither time nor effort to bring about any fundamental changes to the organization.

The problem is not that businesses do not like to or want to change, but it is that they are unable to manage change while maintaining their status quo.

How often have we heard colleagues lament: "I am too busy taking calls from clients" or "I have no time to implement any improvement activities in my department"? This is what is meant by the capacity to change. Change is of no use in its dormancy.

What is required therefore is a complete **paradigm shift.**

What is a Paradigm Shift?[1]

Thomas Kuhn in his Structure of Scientific Revolution introduced the concept of the paradigm shift. He states there that people are not likely to discard an unworkable paradigm, despite many indications that the paradigm is not working properly, until a better paradigm can be presented.

"The decision to reject one paradigm is always simultaneously the decision to accept another, and the judgment leading to that decision involves the comparison of both paradigms with nature and with each other."

Take this scenario for instance. A truck driver, whose employer is contractually bound to deliver haulage in time at an agreed location, will focus on the task at hand – his driving and the destination. An extension of the driver's focus, for example the driver's focus to maintain a performance of consistent on-time delivery (quality) may lead to errors in executing important operational decisions, for example forgoing to stop for fuel. Stopping for fuel here can be seen as the driver's effort to change, which he forgoes (barrier). The effect of this error, which is an empty tank, means that the truck driver succumbs to delays in his delivery at the client's expense (cost).

A paradigm shift can be applied here:

The driver can maintain his performance (focusing at the task at hand) and at the same time make an effort to change (stopping for fuel). The paradigm shift will enable the driver to execute important operational decisions (avoiding any errors) and still meet customer's expectations (the on–time delivery).

Lean Six Sigma can be **the enabler** that achieves this paradigm shift as illustrated below.

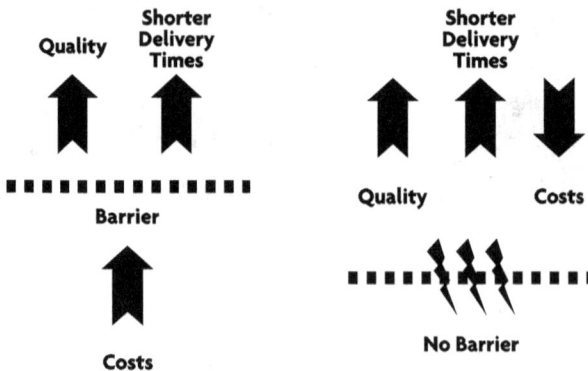

Figure 4.1 : Lean Six Sigma Paradigm Shift[2]

Determined business leaders should use these encounters as lessons to bring about change. Great leaders, including those of successful organizations like GE, Xerox, Motorola and Alcan, have used such experiences as inspiration to adopt and adapt Lean Six Sigma, turning themselves into architects of the future. They know the significance of discovering dormant talent that can entrench change in the DNA of an organization.

"The price of greatness is the responsibility
over each of your thoughts."
– *Sir Winston Churchill*

The Philosophy of Change

Modern businesses can benefit from philosophers and business leaders who have laid out cultural wisdom to awaken the dormant talent.

Ancient philosophy has always advocated change and this can be realised in Thiruvalluvar's *(Thirukural)* philosophy of change and governance and in Sun Tzu's *(Art of War)* philosophy of aggressive growth and expansion.

I–Ching, a great Eastern philosopher, advocated that "change is perpetual in the human world and it is necessary in due time to knowing change and learning to adapt it."[3]

Chinese master Lou Tzu in his text the *Dao De Jing* uses the metaphor of water as the ideal change agent. He says, "water, though soft and yielding, will eventually wear away stone". Lou Tzu emphasizes on the natural, harmonious and steady state of water (change agent) as an imperceptible substance.[5] Heraclitus, a Greek philosopher also uses water as a metaphor of change. He states, "on those stepping into rivers staying the same and other waters flow."

This can be interpreted as follows: the water is the change agent as it needs to flow in order to remain a river. Unwillingness to change can be seen as the water becoming a stagnant pool, like a lake or pond.

An organization aiming to increase its revenue, profits and returns can consider itself as the river and the people that make the changes as the flowing water (the change agents) that can wear away the stone (barriers).

易

"It is hard to be aggressive if you
do not know what your target is."
– *Vince Lombardi, American football coach*

Changing with Strategy and Execution

Most management playbooks and business leaders discuss the need for a strategy to establish a sustainable execution.

An organization that develops a strategy to become the customer's number one choice for its products and services will rightfully develop an execution process with the enabler toolset. The strategy is inspired by change and an enabler toolset – Lean Six Sigma.

The execution process or change management, when applied diligently can harness the highest levels of effectiveness and lead the organization towards expansion and growth.

Change management needs a foundation of focus prior to embarking on the journey towards change and greatness. It is focus that creates positive energy and a positive mindset. This produces a strong and disciplined organization that turns effort into actions and delivers results. Cultivating focus as the foundation creates the courage for change to occur beyond expectation.

Change is a central aspect of human capital development. An organization's dormant talents are its future leaders. They can be discovered and developed towards greatness.

Robin Sharma in his book entitled *The Monk Who Sold His Ferrari* [4] presents several steps for change. Based on his ideas, an organization embracing Lean Six Sigma can adopt a concept of five stepping stones towards greatness.

Stepping Stone 1 – Create a Vision

Creating a clear vision of the organization's goal and target is essential to harness the positive energy and change the mindset. The clearer the vision is, the better the execution process. A clear vision is like a lighthouse navigating business leaders towards greatness.

All successful organizations that have adopted Lean Six Sigma as the enabler started with a clear vision of its goal.

Stepping Stone 2 – Positive Action

Embarking on change often leads to resistance. Hardened traditional paradigms often overwhelm the organization, making it is easy for them to slip back to the status quo and create a resistance to change.

To overcome resistance, the organization must establish positive actions that can drive performance. How often have we observed the project team pulling a rabbit out of the hat (traditional paradigm) a few hours prior to a bid submission? Positive action forces one against the wall to create a positive reaction. This reaction taps into the dormant talents and inspires to achieve outstanding results.

Setting of measurable goals, resolutions, milestones and targets and having these known throughout the organization and its stakeholders, will drive positive action towards achieving them. It will create a critical mass of change agents that a business needs to steer its course towards greatness.

Stepping Stone 3 – Develop a Timeline

A vision cannot materialize if a timeline is not set against its goals, resolution, milestones and targets. Setting of timelines and deadlines attract focus on delivery of results.

Making the vision, timeline and progress visible to everyone in an organization will harness results from the positive action. A typical timeline would include the Initiation Phase, Resource and Project Selection Phase and finally the Execute, Sustain and Evolving Phase.

Implementation Plan

1 Year		Month												
		1	2	3	4	5	6	7	8	9	10	11	12
Initiation	Deployment Design													
	Executive Engagement													
Resource & Project Selection	Champions Sponsors Belt													
	Training Projects													
Execute, Sustain & Evolve	Organization Adaption	Sponsor Workshop	Project & Program Management											
		Executive & Deployment Workshop		BB & BG PRoject Review										
	Black Belt Training													
	Green Belt Training													
	Project Tracking & Validation							$$$$$$$$$$$$$$$$$$$$$$$$$						

INITIATION

Figure 4.2 : Lean Six Sigma Implementation[2]

Stepping Stone 4 – Exert and Exercise

The practice of an enabler tool such as Lean Six Sigma is essential to garner the capacity for change.

Exerting and exercising the use of such a toolset leads to generating positive habits, and positive habits can be easily embedded into the DNA of an organization. The combined effect of creating a vision, having a positive action and developing a timeline generates sufficient spotlight and energy that creates a genetic pathway for the practical and effective use of the Lean Six Sigma toolsets.

The special endeavor exerted to exercise Lean Six Sigma over a period of time will ease itself into a positive daily routine.

Stepping Stone 5 – Achieve and Advance

Achieving a goal set out in a "vision" can be exhilarating. The organization that chooses to adapt change should not forget to fully enjoy the successful results. The failures and experiences along the way are lessons learned towards continuous improvements.

Asian leaders like Dhirubhai Ambani who speaks of "courage and conviction that leads to success" and Nobuyuki Idei who revolutionized the digital age in the Sony Corporation are examples of leaders that achieved and advanced with change.

Change can lead to greatness, if the execution is built on **strategy** and is **led by passion**. Passion is the powerhouse of greatness, the fuel that propels great business leaders to extraordinary success.

Endnotes:
1. *Paradigm Shift (http://en.wikipedia.org/wiki/Paradigm_shift).*
2. *Michael George et al, What is Lean Six Sigma, McGraw-Hill, 2003.*
3. *I-Ching (http://www.taopage.org/iching/philosophy.html).*
4. *Robin Sharma, The Monk Who Sold His Ferrari, Harper One, 1999.*
5. *Lao Tze (http://www.chinapage.com/laotze.html).*

Chapter 5
Organizational Effectiveness

People and mindsets

Every business organization first establishes itself with investments from shareholders and the products and services that are on offer. Then it develops stakeholders and acquires customers. The ultimate aim is to nurture the business into a successful venture that produces results.

At the heart of the business are its people – the shareholders, stakeholders and customers. It is the people who engrain into the business organization the Vision, Mission and Principle Operational Values which guide and steer the workforce to continuously produce results. This means generating results in terms of financial returns i.e. return of invested capital and economic profit.

To achieve results a business organization needs to have its people working effectively as a productive workforce. This can be defined as organizational effectiveness.

Organizational Effectiveness

Organizational effectiveness is essential from the point of inception. It is even more essential when financial results is the determining factor in measuring the success of an organization.

Measuring Success

Measuring success in a business organization usually refers to the success of achieving goals and targets set in the form of financial metrics. Financial metrics can be measured and monitored effectively.

The effectiveness of an organization and its productivity is often inferred from its financial metric. This is because it is often difficult to measure the productivity of a workforce.

Financial results are derived from products and services offered to clients. These products and services are developed, produced and delivered based on a series of activities managed by solidly instituted systems and processes.

In addition to systems and processes, key stakeholders and business drivers will require a strategy or simply a game plan to steer productivity and execute it with a sound workforce. A productive workforce generates products and services of financial value to customers and stakeholders of the business.

In order to attain the desired financial results, the organization must create a culture where employers and employees are not ignorant to the fact that results are achievable when driven by a strategy.

Strategy is a pre-requisite to developing and generating products and services. The execution of strategy is made possible with the existence of institutionalised and measurable systems and processes.

Still, at the heart of it are the people.

UNLOCKING THE HUMAN CAPITAL

Good organizational leaders will ensure that their people are centrally aligned to the organization's vision, mission and values and create a culture of performance that focuses on results. The systems and processes together with the strategy lead and direct the people i.e. the organization's workforce, to deliver results.

Without people, the leaders and the workforce, developing the ability to change and produce results that matter to the customers and stakeholders are hard to achieve. Hence the well known adage: "the soft stuff is the hard stuff!"

Organizational Effectiveness and Lean Six Sigma

Organizational effectiveness is the inner framework that drives the development of change. The culture of change is synonymous to accelerated change and transition that is crucial to an organization that intends to stay ahead of the market competition.

Just like in the mid 1990's, when business organizations in the digital and information age were pushed to change, as Bill Gates put it, "at the speed of thought", business organizations today he states, need to change at the speed of market and competition.

The culture of change, together with an organization's ability to change effectively, is crucial to exert a Lean Six Sigma paradigm shift.

Change enables a continuous improvement culture that identifies the burning platform, goals and targets which the organization requires to improve its offering and position in the competitive market. Thus creating a strategy aimed at results for the customers and stakeholders of the organization.

An institutionalised continuous improvement culture would enable key workforce in the organization to adopt Lean Six Sigma as a solution that unifies the strategy developed from the burning platform with its execution through the DMAIC methodology.

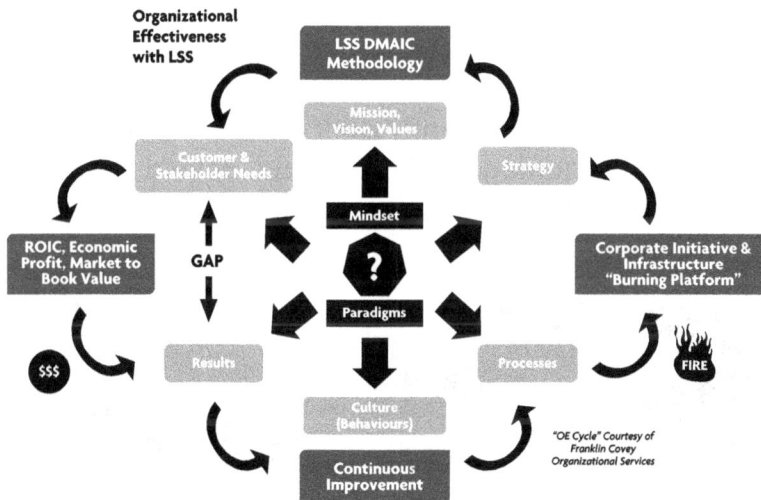

Figure 5.1 : Organizational Effectiveness[1]

The combination of organizational effectiveness, the DMAIC methodology and Lean Six Sigma toolset act as a foundation to establish an enterprise–wide continuous improvement culture.

The rigour established from the methodology will highlight the importance and contribution of all continuous improvement activities. This in turn would improve business performance and ensure that measurable gains are successfully achieved.

The success will narrow the gap between customers or shareholders needs and the results that determine a successful organization.

The change brought by Lean Six Sigma is not just about doing something, it is about doing something *else.* Something that is inherently right, simple and profitable. The key is acquiring an insight and driving people to participate in the operation of an effective and innovative organization.

> "Treat your employees the way
> you want your customers to treat you."
> – *Terry Leahy, CEO of TESCO*

Deploying Lean Six Sigma[2]

Embarking on the deployment of Lean Six Sigma requires the organization's leadership to articulate a clearly defined burning platform and make transition efforts that are aimed at driving and accepting change.

Why deploy Lean Six Sigma?

The purpose of adopting Lean Six Sigma is to utilize it as a process improvement methodology that supports Continuous Improvement and Business Transformation. It trains practitioners to adopt the Lean principles (reducing and eliminating non-value added activities) with the DMAIC methodology (reducing variation, increasing quality) to improve process efficiency and effectiveness. Both manufacturing and transactional processes, for example production, acquisition, logistics, administration and services, can benefit from using Lean Six Sigma.

Organizations typically have departments with various operations and functions. They also have various clients with different types of business and objectives. The deployment of Lean Six Sigma requires standardization and flexibility across the organization. The organization must be functionally and operationally balanced in order to exercise a company wide deployment that will continue to thrive in its culture.

A crucial step is for each organization to establish a corporate Lean Six Sigma structure. This is to be led by a Continuous Improvement Champion, who will be the communication and standardisation linkage between the Lean Six Sigma Team and the management. The Lean Six Sigma structure will comprise specific leadership roles such as Lean Six Sigma Continuous Improvement Council, Deployment Champion, Council Champions, Project Sponsor, Black Belts, Green Belts, Kaizen Leaders and Team Members.

What is the Goal?

The goal is to significantly improve Customer Satisfaction, Operational Costs, Product Quality and Speed. Additionally it is to increase the yield in productivity and revenue. The goal comes from a vision to transform business processes and departmental functions. The vision is to provide value, quality, and responsiveness to customers and reduce cycle time and costs. The goal can be accomplished through a culture of continuous and measurable improvement.

A successful Lean Six Sigma deployment relies on the management to optimize organizational performance. The deployment will address several aspects of organizational effectiveness such as fundamental beliefs and values, organizational infrastructure, education and training, methods and tools and project execution.

Establishing a deployment plan to synchronize, integrate, and manage the execution of Lean Six Sigma is vital to achieve results and financial returns that stakeholders expect. This specific plan will provide the holistic approach necessary to institutionalise Lean Six Sigma in the whole enterprise.

The objective is to have an operational impact through a vigorous approach of identifying processes and products that are no longer relevant, and subsequently eliminating the non-value added operations and activities. It will give an opportunity to generate quick hits and obtain the buy-in from the people to accept change.

A carefully thought out deployment plan can minimize the impact of ever expanding customer's requirements whilst developing a competitive advantage. This will support the operations, divest functions that are no longer relevant for the operational environment and re-engineer processes to increase responsiveness and satisfaction to customers.

Eight Guiding Principles of Lean Six Sigma

The mindset to continuously improve applies to the deployment and management of Lean Six Sigma. A successful deployment can be achieved by following a set of guiding principles. These guiding principles are ideas that apply to the deployment since the management of a deployment is in itself a process. Processes, should always be designed with flexibility in mind and the ability to periodically introduce and review controlled and measurable changes.

Customer Centricity

Knowledge and deep understanding of what the customer values most is the primary guiding principle. The foundation of this understanding is the successful completion of the "Voice of the Customer" and "Value Stream" analysis, which will determine areas and opportunities for improvement. Creation of Value Stream Maps that define the suppliers, inputs and outputs of a process, the products and services flow, the resource commitment, the cycle time, information flow and customers is an important first Lean Six Sigma task.

What is a Value Stream Map?

The Value Stream Map is an information rich process flow diagram that identifies and displays all key process steps (both value added and non-value added) beginning with the supplier and ending with the customer. It incorporates the communication flow, material flow, inventories and lead time, allowing managers to see and recognize deficiencies in the end-to-end flow of both material and information as a product (or service) makes its way through the process.

Engaging Process Owners and Sponsors

The Senior Management team and the Continuous Improvement Champion have to demonstrate proactive engagement and visible participation in Lean Six Sigma as it is deployed throughout the organization. This is the second guiding principle. Commitment is demonstrated from the very beginning, in their active involvement in the upfront decisions of "who", "what", "where", "when", and "how" in overseeing and guiding the Process Owners and Sponsors of continuous improvement projects.

Process Owners and Sponsors are engaged by making them accountable to the success or failure of the projects and making the execution of the projects their priority. To achieve an effective organizational change, leaders must own the changes and improvements to business processes and maintain accountability for results. It is critical to maintain the roles and responsibilities, especially for the Project Sponsors and Process Leads contributing to project effectiveness.

Setting of two-year and five-year performance goals that reflect gains in operating efficiencies and financial performance in a way that is consistent with the organization's goals and objective is a guiding principle for deployment. The process owners and sponsors team are central to the Lean Six Sigma organizational structure and much of the success lies on them being engaged in the transition process.

Operational Results

The third guiding principle is to ensure that projects or continuous improvement efforts will only be undertaken when there is evidence indicating that changes will result in tangible and quantifiable operational improvements. Activities and process steps that are determined by customers to be "non-value-added" from their perspective provide material opportunities for improvement. The goal is to identify command processes that are the most mission critical, which can provide the greatest operational, readiness, and financial benefits, and which can be most readily improved by the Lean principles and tool sets.

Resource Commitment

> ## Resource Commitment
> "Far Sighted Companies will find ways to endear themselves to their staff, who would respond by improving productivity and work quality. These companies would do the same in terms of the customers and the community in which they operate."
> – *Hafidz Mahpar, What's the Big Idea (The Star, December 2008).*

The fourth principle is to allocate a significant number of personnel to devote on a full-time basis to the Lean Six Sigma efforts. The number of practitioners in the organization will be composed of at least 3% to 5% of full-time staff. Other employees and command personnel can also regularly participate in Lean Six Sigma improvement projects on a part-time basis.

The management must consider adopting a 5 step approach as illustrated below to ensure that critical resources are committed to projects that are aligned to the critical business needs and are prioritised based on benefit and effort criteria that in turn will provide a platform towards a successful adoption and implementation of Lean Six Sigma.

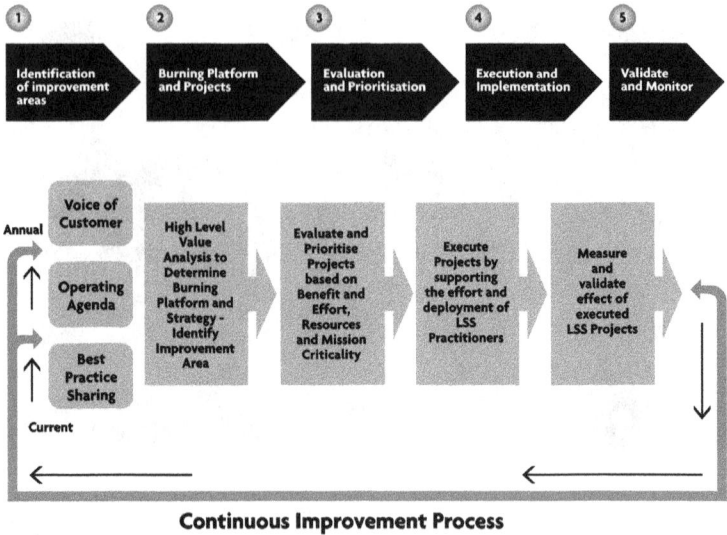

Continuous Improvement Process

Figure 5.2 : Continuous Improvement Process[3]

Rigorous Project Selection

The fifth guiding principle is to establish and maintain a project pipeline that addresses key areas of opportunity. The initial wave projects should follow a top–down approach that identifies and prioritises projects based on expected benefit to the organization versus expected effort to complete the project. Going forward, the organization will establish a process that best supports its goals and future state vision.

Matching of Problem and Approach

Lean Six Sigma provides a flexible approach to problem solving that matches the approach to the complexity of the project. This is the sixth guiding principle.

Using Kaizen events, or Rapid Improvement Events (RIEs), for relatively straightforward problems, a team of 5 to 8 people can reasonably attack this type of problem over a period of 5 days, not including preparation time before the event or time afterward to tie up loose ends. Kaizen teams can be used for 5 to 30 day projects with an experienced facilitator or Kaizen Leaders trained in Lean tools and principles to lead the RIE.

A Green Belt project typically requires between 1 to 3 months to perform with little or no additional time for preparation or follow-up. Such projects fall within the Green Belt's organization and do not span multiple organizations. Every Green Belt will be trained on the basic use of Lean Six Sigma toolset and the fundamentals of statistical approach of problem solving.

A Black Belt Project typically requires 3 to 6 months to perform with substantial time for preparation and engagement across divisions and organization. A Black Belt would be trained with a complete Lean Six Sigma toolset including advanced statistical problem solving methods. Black Belts would be trained and coached with projects that would result in a distinct or direct measurable return to the organization.

Minimal "Projects in Progress"

The seventh guiding principle is for the Deployment Champion to actively restrict the number of projects in process, and focus on rapid completion. Organizations often push for as many continuous improvement projects as possible into the pipeline in an effort to produce results failing to bear in mind the limited resources. This approach increases the time to project completion project and causes delays in realising bottom-line results.

The best number of projects in process depends on the number of active change agents, availability of team members, and the organization's experience level with Lean Six Sigma. During the initial stages of deployment, it is better to limit each team or change agent to one project at a time.

Results Tracking Process

The eighth guiding principle is to establish a thorough results tracking process. It is important to track results for projects and use that information to improve the Lean Six Sigma deployment. Best practices are to be shared throughout the organization. Each project will include a Define phase that sets project goals and a Control Phase that measures results. Organizations are recommended to use project monitoring and management system, such as Proj X or Power Steering, to track and report results.

Endnotes:

1. Stephen R Covey, Principle Centered Leadership, Free Press,1992
   and Mr. Sitham, FranklinCovey Malaysia, Discussion Notes, Nov 2006.

2. Michael L George, Lean Six Sigma, McGraw–Hill, 2002.

3. UMS Training and Consulting, UMS Consulting GmbH Course Notes,
   Frankfurt, Germany , Jan 2007.

Chapter 6
Changing with Lean Six Sigma

From Carrot-Stick to Trim Tab

FW Taylor, the father of the Scientific Management Theory, believed that throughout the Industrial Age, motivation in the workplace was driven by money.

Business organizations employed an extensive use of the "carrot-and-stick" theory of motivation. The "carrot-and-stick" approach led its hardworking members towards rewards and imposed a penalty on workers who failed to achieve work expectations.

A comparison of this approach can be made to the infamous "20-70-10" management theory that was embedded into the GE culture, where the "carrot" drove the performance of the 20-70 portion of the organization and the "stick" used on the 10.

Nevertheless, the "carrot–and–stick" theory succeeded in increasing the productivity of various industries by 50-fold. It was a mindset and to a certain extent, this mindset is still in use in today's business environment.

Industrial Age to Information Age[1]

The world today has swiftly moved away from the Industrial Age to the Information Age. Over more than a century, the experience of the Industrial Age has brought about modernization and development processes driven by technological innovation. The values that define these innovations include skills and abilities to control processes and to make it efficient.

The Information Age, on the other hand focuses on empowering the Knowledge Worker and to set free the vast potential of latent or dormant creative talents and capabilities. What the knowledge worker wants is the choice to lead in an environment of dynamic globalization. In order for them to lead, they need to enhance their skills and become sensitive to the processes that define voices of customers and business.

Industrial Age   Information Age

Quality and Value in the Service Industry

Service industries today include banking and financial institutions, shared services and operations, insurance services, travel and logistic services, etc. These industries have two major processes that enable the provision of value-add to the services in offer. The first is the customer-facing processes, e.g. call centers, hospitality, internet retails, health care and pharmaceuticals. The second is the internal business processes, e.g. training, recruitment, invoicing, billing, material replenishments, shared services and deliveries. These are the processes that produce the voices of customer and the voices of business, and become the quality and value drivers in the service industries.

A problem typically faced by the service industry is constraints that impede the flexibility to stratify customer requests and demands, due to the incapability of front line service centers.

Naturally, all requests are processed in a queue-like manner resulting in delays in delivery of materials, information or services to locations where urgency is required. Non-urgent requests are processed in advance, probably in batches and delivered to locations that have no urgent needs. The execution of this process ultimately results in costs to be incurred both at the front-end and the back-end operations, as well as at the customer's location. This is an example of non-value add activities or waste.

Another problem is when non-conformity exists. When products or services fail to conform to a customer's demand, it becomes a defect, and all efforts spent in terms of time, resources, materials and costs are wasted.

> "Any intelligent fool can make things bigger,
> more complex and more violent.
> It takes a touch of genius – and a lot of
> courage – to move in the opposite direction."
> – *Albert Einstein*

There is a price to pay for non-conformity. For an organization, it means it has produced work or service that a customer is not willing to pay for. This ultimately drives the customer away to an alternate provider for similar products or services. The voice of customer is only heard when the defect occurs, in the form of complaints whilst the voice of the business fails to focus on the process value stream that identifies the root cause.

On the other hand, non-conformity or waste can help organizations identify and prioritise their improvement actions. Every problem is an opportunity. The opportunity requires the utilisation of resources and concentration on improving the activities or processes that affect customers' needs. The improvement should result in "getting things done right the first time".

These are opportunities often seen by the Knowledge Worker, who can benefit from the vigorous toolset that Lean Six Sigma offers, to enable an Information Age paradigm shift.

Trim–Tab[1]

> ### Buckminster Fuller's analogy of a trim–tab[2]
>
> "Something hit me very hard once, thinking about what one little man could do. Think of the Queen Mary – the whole ship goes by and then comes the rudder. And there's a tiny thing at the edge of the rudder called a trim tab.
>
> It's a miniature rudder. Just moving the little trim tab builds a low pressure that pulls the rudder around. Takes almost no effort at all. So I said that the little individual can be a trim tab. Society thinks it's going right by you, that it's left you altogether. But if you're doing dynamic things mentally, the fact is that you can just put your foot out like that and the whole big ship of state is going to go.
>
> So I said, call me Trim Tab."

The foundation of the Information Age is the Knowledge Worker. From here a culture of talents can develop and once aligned to the goals of a business organization, it can establish a winning mindset. A mindset that is determined to unleash more intelligence, more capability, more creativity and more proactive ability than the work requires or allows.

It enables people engagement and their contribution that results in the continuous development and growth of an organization where everyone who is a part of it will benefit. The foundation of this is the knowledge worker, the trim tab.

Paradigm Shift in the Information Age

What is the paradigm shift that is required in the Information Age?

Lean Six Sigma is a scientific value of data driven decision making and the analytical thought process of problem solving. It is the single most effective problem-solving methodology, which eliminates root-causes and with sustainable solutions, drives not only organizational performances, but also the fundamental values of a business: revenue growth, operating profit and book to market value. Lean Six Sigma's strategy is to maximize the returns to the shareholder.

Today, it is not only the manufacturing industry that relies on information to gain competitive advantage but a whole slew of service industries that thrives on information and knowledge from processes, markets, customers needs and value.

Call centers, outsourcing service providers, financial retailers, insurance and logistics are examples of service based industries that rely on knowledge workers to generate 70% to 80% of value add to goods and services provided to its customers. Each Knowledge Worker is empowered to effect, enable and sustain significant change regardless of his or her position in the organization.

Lean Six Sigma, a key skill set for today's generation of Knowledge Workers, enables the creation and release of countless and effortless trim tabs. One can imagine the gains that can be achieved if an entire knowledge workforce is made Lean Six Sigma literate. Enabling an entire workforce of trim tabs, with optimism and effort, significant gains can be achieved.

This paradigm shift can lead to a further 50 fold increase in productivity with no significant effort in terms of financial and human capital i.e. without the carrot or the stick.

Lean Six Sigma is the rudder that steers the organization forward.

Endnotes:
1. Stephen R. Covey, Foreword in Six Sigma for Dummies
   by Craig Gygi, For Dummies, 2005.
2. Buckminster Fuller Institute
   (http://www.bfi.org/our_programs/publications/trimtab).
3. George Group Consulting, Alcan–George Group Lean Six Sigma Course
   Notes, Nov 2003.

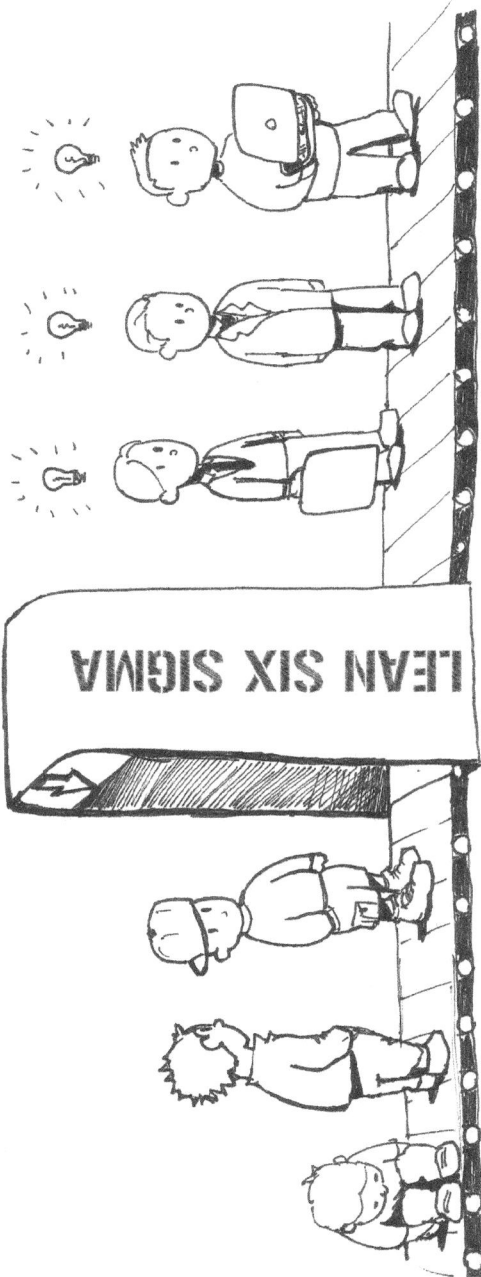

Changing with Lean Six Sigma

Section THREE

Lean Six Sigma, The Asian Experience

Chapter 7
Industrial Case Study

Increasing Productivity in Manufacturing[1]
The following case study is based on an experience with a manufacturing facility that produces raw material supply for the packaging industry. The manufacturer uses a propriety process and has for sometime undergone a productivity problem. Lean Six Sigma was chosen as the methodology in order to identify a permanent solution.

The production's capability did not meet the customer's demand for raw material supply. At the time of the study, the mean value for daily production was 98.5 Metric Tonnes (MT) of raw material. Prior to the project, the market demand was greater than the average daily productivity and this demand was only met by importing substitute raw material products from a sister plant overseas at a premium cost.

This study describes the activities and the thought processes that were undertaken throughout the DMAIC phases to identify the solutions.

DEFINE Phase

The Lean Six Sigma project was launched by assembling a team that was led by a Black Belt. The project team consisted of production team supervisors, a planning supervisor, a client technical supervisor and an engineering supervisor. The project was sponsored by the production manager (also the process owner) who had profit and loss accountability for the manufacturing department.

The define phase was launched and the objective was to complete four critical elements that would ensure that the project was Specific, Measureable, Attainable, Realistic and Time-bound (SMART). These elements were:

1. Charter with a problem statement and goal statement
2. Team on-boarding and launch
3. SIPOC (Supplier Input Process Output Customer) diagram
4. Voice of Customer and Voice of Business

The most important aspect of the define phase was a statement that defined only the problem that needed to be solved and no solutions or implementation plans were described with the problem.

Charter

• **Problem Statement:**

– Tier 1 department is not producing enough materials to meet customer demand. The 2003 daily production mean was about 98.5MT. The problem originally surfaced in the year 2000 when sales demanded more output, however with the current capability, it limits the overall productivity output. The pain is having to import raw materials from the sister plant at a premium cost in order to maintain customer satisfaction.

• **Goal Statement:**

– The goal is to increase the average daily productivity output by an extra 10% (9MT) and to yield an economic profit of USD$400 per annum.

Figure 7.1 : Project Charter – Problem and Goal Statement

In addition to the Charter, the project scope was determined by using a tool known as SIPOC (Supplier – Input – Process – Output – Customer). The Voices of Customers and Business were identified and validated by the project teams. These voices were translated to Critical To Customers (CTC) or Cost Of Poor Quality (COPQ) elements and were specified as a measureable metric. The outputs based on these tools are shown in the subsequent illustrations.

SIPOC DIAGRAM

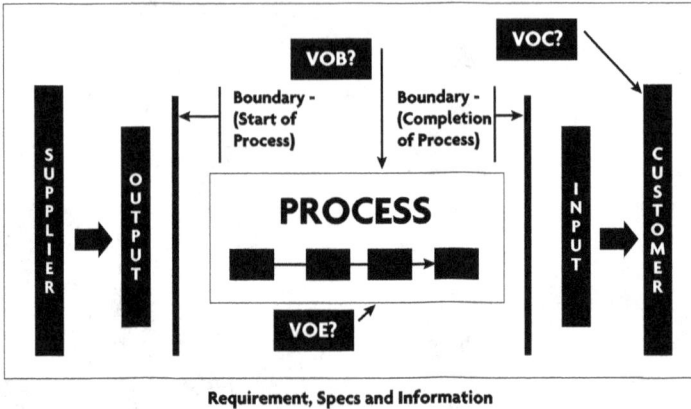

Requirement, Specs and Information

Figure 7.2 : SIPOC Diagram – Project Scope Limited to the boundary of process inputs and outputs

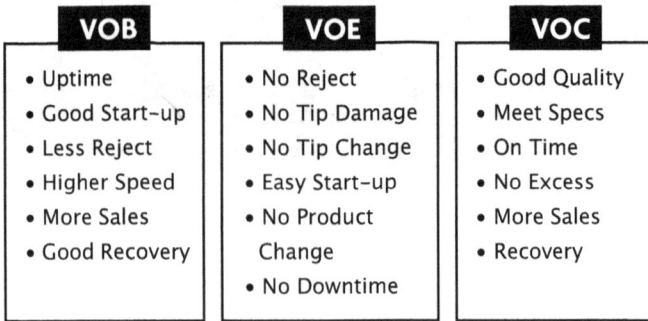

VOB	VOE	VOC
• Uptime	• No Reject	• Good Quality
• Good Start–up	• No Tip Damage	• Meet Specs
• Less Reject	• No Tip Change	• On Time
• Higher Speed	• Easy Start–up	• No Excess
• More Sales	• No Product	• More Sales
• Good Recovery	Change	• Recovery
	• No Downtime	

Figure 7.3 : Voices that Matter – Voice of Business, Voice of Employees & Voice of Customer

At the end of the Define phase, a gate review was conducted. This formal review was held with the project sponsor. The aim was to reach a consensus on the goals and targets of the project with facts from the SIPOC and Voices of the Business and Customer. The gate review was an important milestone in DMAIC cycle before progressing to the next phase.

MEASURE Phase

The key goal of the Measure phase was to establish a measurement baseline with respect to the metric established from the COPQ elements. A data collection plan was developed to determine the type of data that was required, the source and its location. The data collection plan also identified the data collector, how the data could be collected and when it was required.

In this project, data was required to show a baseline performance measure on productivity, quality and product quantity by raw material classification. Any improvements achieved can be gauged against the baseline.

As the data relied heavily on the accuracy of the measurement device in use and the effectiveness of the data collector, the team realized that the accuracy and precision of the data needed validation using a technique known as Measurement System Analysis.

Measurement System Analysis determines the amount of variability induced in the data that originated from the measurement process (Repeatability). This technique, commonly known as Gage R&R, was also used to determine the errors that could potentially affect the accuracy of the data when the measurement process was conducted by different operators or by the same operators at different instances (Reproducibility).

Once the measurement system was validated, a baseline performance was established. This baseline data was presented graphically to simplify the information and establish a common method of visual understanding. The baseline data also established the extent of the problem.

Examples of baseline data include capability analysis, time series plots and a Pareto chart that was developed to stratify potential problem areas. With this baseline data, potential quick wins and critical focus areas were identified using the empirical 80–20 rule.

This rule states that 80% of the issues (effects) at hand could be resolved by addressing 20% of the problems (causes). These graphical interpretations of data and capability measurements were determined using the statistical software package called MINITAB. Examples of data presented graphically as outputs of the measure phase are shown in Figure 7.4.

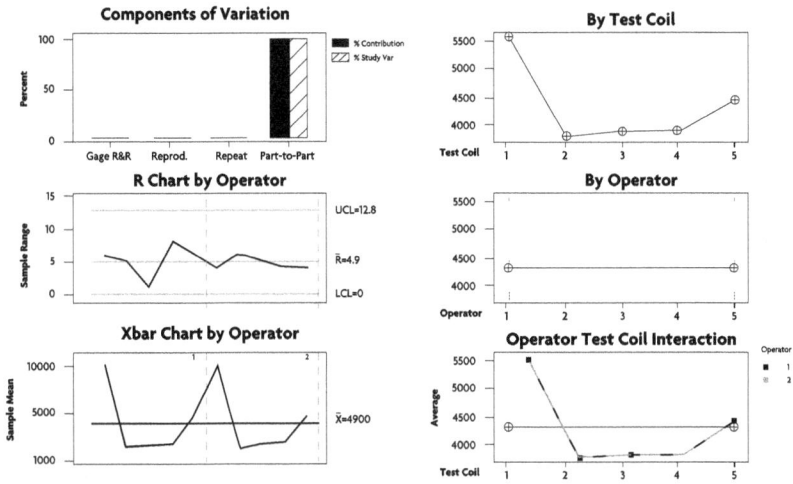

Figure 7.4 : Gage R&R – Study of Repeatability & Reproducibility

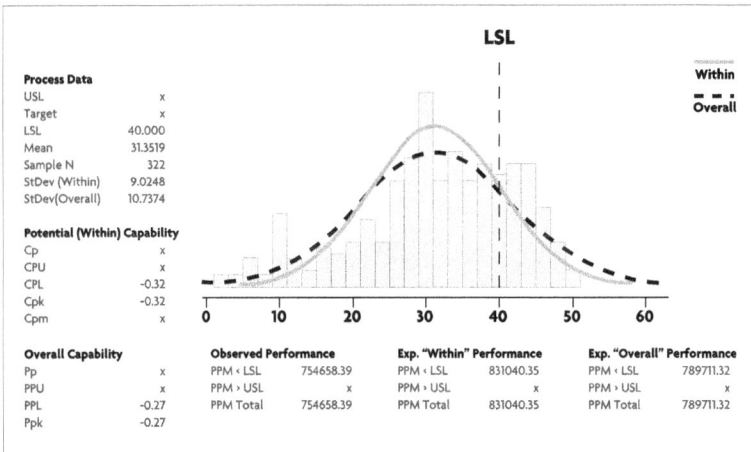

Figure 7.5 : Histogram – Process Capability Baseline

ANALYSE Phase

The goal of the Analyse Phase was to identify the critical few root causes (from the trivial many reasons that were perceived to be the cause when the problem was first Defined). A cause and effect relationship between the input variables and output variables was established to validate the critical few root causes.

The Analyse Phase approach was having a brainstorming session to generate potential root causes by using the Cause & Effect diagram or better known as the 'Fishbone' Ishikawa diagram. Ideas of potential root causes gathered from the Ishikawa diagram were organized into a Cause & Effect Matrix using a method known as KJ Analysis (affinity analysis and diagrams). This Matrix was used to narrow down and determine the impact of those potential root causes to the production output.

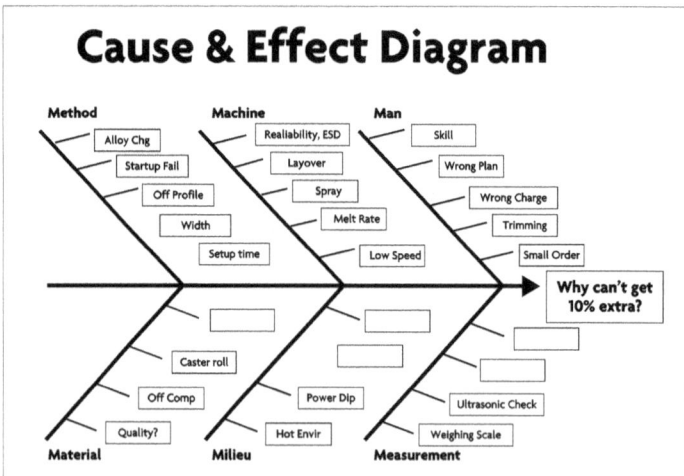

Figure 7.6 : Ishikawa Diagram – Brainstorming ideas

Statistical methods were utilized to validate the identified potential root causes. Validation of these root causes gave a clear focus on the 'critical root cause'. It provided the team with ideas on what needed to be improved.

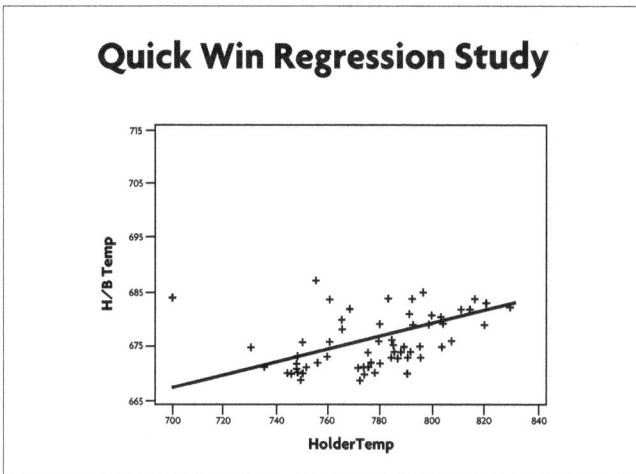

Quick Win Regression Study

Figure 7.7 : Simple Regression – Correlating Input to Output Measures

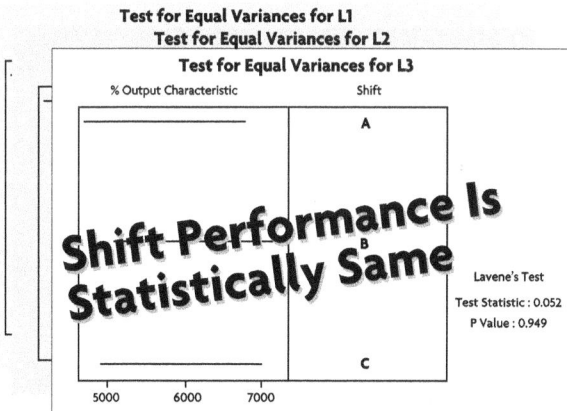

Shift Performance

Test for Equal Variances for L1
Test for Equal Variances for L2
Test for Equal Variances for L3

% Output Characteristic   Shift

A

Shift Performance Is Statistically Same

B

Lavene's Test
Test Statistic : 0.052
P Value : 0.949

C

5000   6000   7000

Figure 7.8 : Analysis of Variance – Analysing the effect of input variation

IMPROVE Phase

Statistical tests that validated the 'critical root causes' required the team to analyse the effects of key input process variables. The data that validated the root causes and effects led the team to choose optimization and to improve the interactions of input and output variables as the solution.

This solution required the use of Design of Experiments, an advanced statistical tool that is able to analyse the effect and interactions of various critical process variables simultaneously. The tool not only reduced the time required to conduct the studies, but was easily incorporated during the production process. The goal of this study was to identify the optimal process parameters that would reduce the defects from the production process.

DOE Analysis

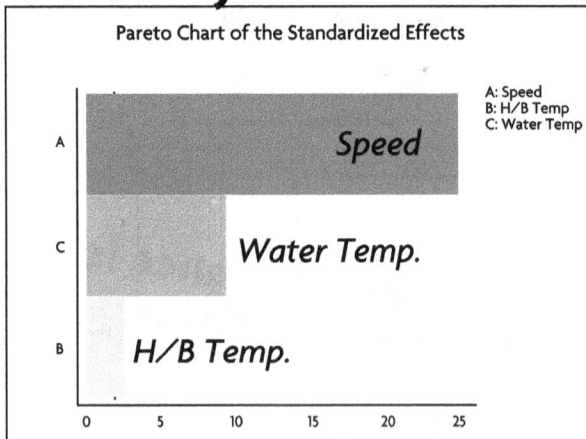

Figure 7.9 : DOE – The Speed effect

The Design of Experiments study rapidly identified the critical process variable and the optimization parameters. The process optimization enabled the team to meet the improvement goals.

Based on this result, a pilot implementation was planned to be incorporated in the production process. The optimized parameters were tested in a controlled manner in the production environment.

Prior to the implementation, the pilot production team was thoroughly debriefed. A pilot implementation plan was prepared. A Gantt-chart and communication plan was developed. Draft Standard-Operating-Procedures and Work-Instructions were prepared and communicated to the production teams, process owner and stakeholders.

A data collection plan was also prepared to measure the key process variable for comparison to the baseline established in the Measure Phase. Finally, results from the pilot implementation were gathered and presented graphically.

DOE Analysis...*cont.*

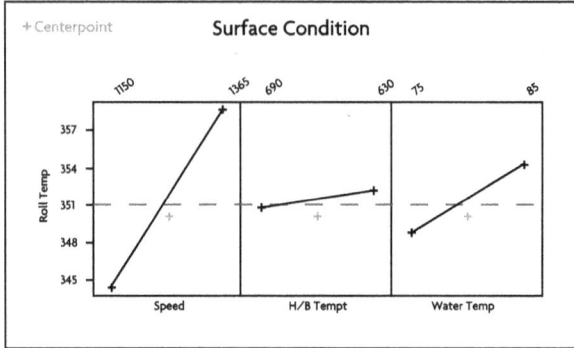

Figure 7.10 : DOE - The optimized process parameters

CONTROL Phase

The success of a control pilot enabled the team to progress into the final DMAIC cycle – the Control Phase. This phase was predominantly about documenting and handing over the improvement to the process owner. The process owner would then implement the solution and sustain the gains that were demonstrated in the pilot.

To facilitate the final implementation, finalised Standard Operating Procedures, Work Instruction, Monitoring and Reaction Plans were reviewed and documented. Control charts for process monitoring were established using the measures identified in the DMAIC cycle.

Keeping those vital process input variables under control and maintaining the optimized parameters was the key to sustaining the gains.

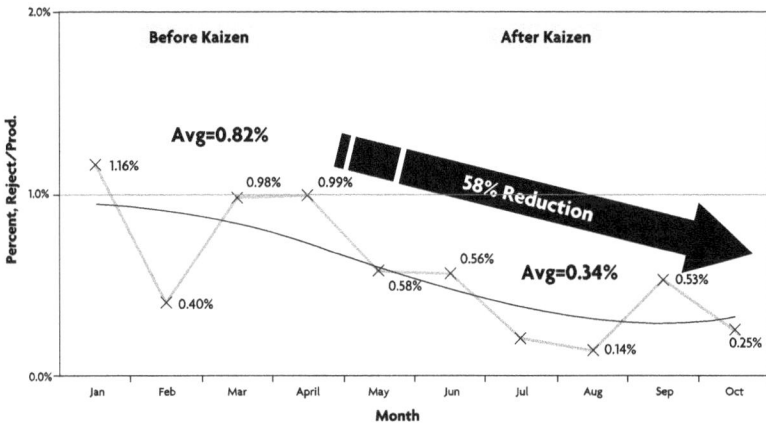

Figure 7.11 : Monitoring Plan – Taking stock of the improvement

After a period of three to six months, the sustainability of the optimization was reviewed and validated. Statistical tests were again used to check for significant improvements to the baseline. In this project the production mean improved from 98.5MT to 106.7MT and daily productivity variation was reduced. As a result the production was statistically stable and in control. In terms of financial benefit, the improvement contributed about US$400,000 annually in revenue.

Chapter 8

Integrating Lean Six Sigma into Financial Services[1]

Eliminating Waste & Improving Services

Picture this scenario: several stacks of loan application forms enter a consumer loans department in a commercial bank. Imagine the paper trail. Application forms jump from one officer's desk to another, go up and down floors in the elevator, before reaching the department for approval and finally to the front office where it is handed over to the applicant, who may be a potential customer.

The paper trail at times can be an astonishing few kilometers long if one were to physically trace through the value stream. Let's face it, it's hard to believe!

"Everyone in all the departments is working hard but why does it still take too long to process an application?" Everyone but the client sees it as real work. "Why does it take so long to make a decision?" asks the applicant, who is the potential customer.

Today, most financial institutions are turning to process improvement methodologies to improve the speed of operation. This study in a consumer loans department shows how a simple Lean Principle on identifying and eliminating waste can be used to improve the speed of services.

The aim is to identify value-adding (for customers) and value-enabling steps (for businesses) in the activities that each is willing to pay for when identified. Everything else is recognized as waste. Waste in this aspect is the loss of time, resources and costs that cannot be recovered – often known as the hidden costs.

What is Waste?
Lean trains the practitioners to develop the intelligence to "sense" waste. Practitioners are trained to recognize waste that frequently manifest physically and virtually in any process and to categorize them by three main elements.

1. Muda – Non-Value Added Work
- Non-value adding work is waste, i.e. activities that are undertaken based on the present work establishment.

- Muda requires processes or activities to be distinguished as value adding, value enabling and non-value add.

2. Muri – Unreasonable Work

- All the unreasonable work that management imposes on workers because of poor organization such as carrying heavy weights, moving things around, dangerous tasks, etc.

- It is pushing a person or a machine beyond its natural limits and is almost always a cause of variation.

3. Mura – Unbalanced or Variation

- Increase in demand which causes the need to squeeze extra productivity from the process which causes routines and standards to be modified or stretched.

- This stretch and improvisation leads to "Muri" style waste which leads to mistakes, corrections, backflow and waiting, which creates "Muda".

Waste comes in many forms. Lean names them as the "7 Deadly Wastes". They are Transportation, Inventory, Motion, Waiting, Over-processing, Over-production and Defects

Figure 8.1 : Types of Waste

What is Transportation?

Any unnecessary movement of materials, products, documents or information can be described as "transportation" waste. In transactional services, this is reflected by activities that transfer (or handovers) from one individual to another, within departments or between departments, which adds time to the overall process. In the service environment, this manifests itself as tasks to be collected and delivered, physically or virtually (electronic data transfers, e.g. processes involving multiple share service center sites).

Each time an activity is transferred or moved, it is exposed to the risks of being delayed, lost or done incorrectly. This results in inefficiencies that become inherent in the process.

Eliminating transportation can at one extreme result in the combination of tasks or the other extreme result in the relocating or redirecting of tasks to minimize the physical or virtual movement.

What is Inventory?

It is the work-in-process, or incomplete work, that does not meet the demand rate or the expected completion time of the customer. Inventory can be considered as "hyper-tension", an invisible problem to the financial services. It is the physical piles of unattended inboxes, lists of pending enquiries or emails or time a client spends in a queue.

Having unattended inboxes also relates to having incurred the expense of time and cost of resource for work not done. In other words capital spent that is not producing revenue. Transactional activities that are not actively processed is non value add and is a waste.

The goal is to have the sufficient inventory for immediate and short-term needs. Ignoring process inventory drives up cost- investing into additional resources or larger virtual storage capacities. These are some examples of effects when inventory is not seriously considered.

"Working Hard or Hardly Working?

What is Motion?

It is the unnecessary movement of people or resources. The physical movement of personnel from a station to another to continue a process is an example of motion. Another example is switching between computer terminals or databases, which is a form of motion that requires additional steps to be executed before a true value–adding step can be carried out. Motion in the transactional world is often a result of Transportation and Inventory.

Picture this scenario: A customer walks into a bank and makes a complaint to the Front Desk officer. In an effort to resolve this fresh complaint and attend to a queue of outstanding complaints (inventory), the officer incompletes the task of logging the complaint into an information system. Due to the nature of the complaint, it is escalated to the supervising officers located in a different level of the building (transportation). Subsequently, when the customer makes a status check at a different time, the new Front Desk officer attending the customer would end up spending unwanted time searching and sorting (motion) through for information regarding the complaint.

In this case, both transportation and inventory caused motion. Motion resulted in the time taken to resolve a complaint to be extended at the customer's expense.

What is Waiting?

Waiting is the elapsed time between the end of a process step (or activity) and the beginning of another. Waiting may have a direct or indirect impact on the customer. The time spent waiting between processes (or activities) results in customers having to wait for the delivery of a product or service.

A typical example of waiting in a financial institution is the time taken to return an approved document or requisition. For example financial processes that require multiple approvals, e.g. purchase requisition or loan disbursement to customers. Waiting is a waste that can potentially halt the flow of processes and affect productivity. Employees that are responsible to execute specific activities will have an empty workstation. They may end up waiting until the necessary steps in the preceding processes are completed. In this case, the approvals of requisitions or disbursements.

This is one of the deadly wastes in processes as there is always the possible existence of a competitor who can deliver products and services quicker according to customers' expectation.

Techniques such as handover analysis, functional deployment maps and value stream maps are potent in identifying the wastes such as Motion and Waiting, which are typical causes of delays.

What is Over-Processing?

Over-Processing means adding more work to a product or a service than necessary and trying to exceed the customers' requirement. This translates to adding more perceived "value" to a product or the service. "Value" that a customer is not willing to pay for.

An example of over-processing which affects customers of financial services is the cost of service charges for statements. Financial institutions by default send customers a hard copy financial statement and charge a fee for this service. Customers that utilize internet banking and who have the ability to review the financial transactions as often as possible would consider the service charge non-value add. For the institution, all the activities that are undertaken in the process of preparing and posting the statement to the customer is redundant and can be considered as Over-processing.

Another example of over-processing in financial institutions is the inclusion of promotional and general marketing information with monthly bank statements. This is quite common for a customer who receives credit card statements via mail. The mail is often filled with glossy booklets and pamphlets. Not all customers would pay attention to this information.

Most of them would only review the information that matters - the credit card statement and the rest of the information pack would be discarded as waste. Over-processing occurs in this context as the service provider does not clearly understand the customer's need. The standardised marketing and promotional process incurs additional cost (printing and postage for example) often with poor rates of returns.

What is Over-Production?

Over-Production is the use of capacity and capability beyond the mean of the present service or product requirement, resulting in outputs that are not delivered to customers. In simple terms, it can be viewed as the production or acquisition of material or information before it is actually required.

An example of over-production in the financial services is when a procurement department is processing a batch of printed material requests for several of its front line service centers. When the existing process does not allow the flexibility of understanding requests and demands based on actual need, then all requests would be processed in a queue like manner.

This results in delays of delivery of materials to locations where urgency is required. Non-urgent requests would be processed in advance and potentially in batches and delivered to locations that have no existing present needs, resulting in the need to manage the inventory of additional printed materials.

Over-production, in a sense, is work carried out ahead of the customers' need and can also result in wastes as the services are performed without a clear understanding of the customer's requirement. Over-production hides the effectiveness of true productivity. It creates the "just-in-case" behaviour which causes costs to be incurred unnecessarily.

Just-In-Time   Just-In-Case

What is Defect?

Defect, is always seen when there is non-conformity. When products or services do not conform to a customer's demand, then it becomes a defect. All effort in terms of time, resources, and materials are wasted costs that are incurred to realize the product or service. Non-conformity comes with a price.

A common example of Defect in financial institutions is loan defaulters. Institutions that issue loans without adhering to a standardised applicant assessment process such as credit checks are often exposed to the risk of having to manage defaulters. The balance between resources to manage defaulters and the risk of defaulters is not thoroughly established. This is the failure to understand the voice of business and the cost of poor quality.

In this scenario, the voice of business is only heard when a defect occurs, in the form of increased cost of recovery (defaulted loans). The resulting effect is the institution engaging reactively to improve the debt recovery process, and failing to focus on the process value stream to identify where the defect originally occurred i.e. the approval process. Eliminating the root cause of a defect presents a lasting solution to eliminating the very occurrence of the defect.

For the financial institution as a whole, it has produced work or service that allows defects to be processed through its value stream. By the time a defect is identified, it has incurred the costs to produce the product or service, at the institution's expense. If the rate of producing defects is high, then inadvertently the cost of producing a product or service that meets the customers' requirement is high.

For an intelligent customer, it is a cost he or she would not be willing to pay and ultimately it drives them to see an alternate provider for the products and services.

Eliminating TIMWOOD

The wastes that are described here is know as the acronym TIMWOOD. Lean trains its practitioners to be aware of TIMWOOD and eliminate it. Having TIMWOOD eliminated from the processes, products and services will extend their value-added elements that meet the customers' requirements and demand. Eliminating TIMWOOD does not only improve operational performance but also drives the cost of time, resources and productivity down – an important value that can be passed over to the customers.

Endnotes:

1. Bill Kastle, Learning to Recognize Process Waste in Financial Services at www.isixsigma.com.
   (http://finance.isixsigma.com/library/contenct/c040324a.asp)

Chapter 9

Sustaining a Deployment

Lean Six Sigma at your Service

> "Disciplines, structured logical techniques,
> along with knowledge sharing with coaches,
> and measurement will bring positive results.
> The results are enhanced if management
> steps up and supports its people."
> – *Gary Cone, Thoughts About the New Six Sigma.*

"Six Sigma is like a trip to the dentist", says Jack Welch. Every leader that envisions success to the extent achieved by GE will follow Jack's playbook:
"Incorporate Lean Six Sigma into the organization".

It begins with the leader selecting a reputable external consulting team to design the deployment and roll out a structured program. The roll out involves a period of anywhere between nine to eighteen months or sometimes even more depending on the size of the deployment.

From the outset the external Lean Six Sigma consulting team will ensure that a sustainability structure is established and executed. This structure is extremely important, especially when the consulting team is no longer around to guide and coach the Sponsors, Champions and the Black Belts and to ensure that the Lean Six Sigma program continues to sustain the delivery of results.

The following case study describes the sustainability activities that were undertaken by the management of a services division. Its aim was to ensure that the Lean Six Sigma methodology was embedded to become the DNA of the organization. Essentially, the goal was to sustain the change that was producing results.

A Case Study on Sustaining Change in a Financial Services Organization

Sustaining change requires effort. An effort that has to be continuous, but, sustaining and continuous could mean the same thing. How did the organization distinguish between "sustaining" change and "continuous" change? How did they make it work without turning it into a monumental task?

The first step was to make change a familiarity in the organization. Change was made to look and feel like a brand. "One has to give it a name and if possible its own image, logo, fonts, colors, theme, etc. Examples are brand names like Lean Transformation, First Choice, Maximizing Value, i-Six Sigma and Sony Six Sigma. These are brands that reflect the management's drive and resolve to make Lean Six Sigma synonymous to the organization. Everyone, including employers, employees and customers, had to at the very least be familiar with the name that meant change.

The second step was to establish a conceptual process for sustaining the change. Without a sustainability process in place, effort put into maintaining the successes of Lean Six Sigma would not have yielded the DNA embedding results. An example of a sustainability process used by this financial services organization is shown below. The process can be visualized as the effort to plant and grow a fruit tree.

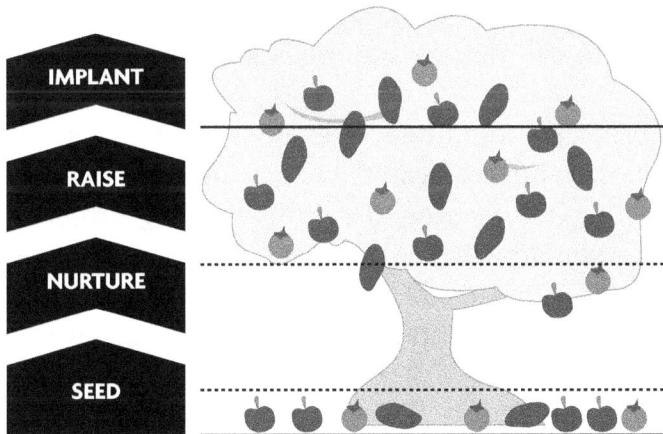

Figure 9.1 : Lean Six Sigma Sustainability Tree

SEED Phase: Awareness is raised and knowledge is disseminated and spread throughout the management and the organization. The burning platform and the impact on day-to-day business are effectively articulated.

In this phase, the organization engages its senior and regional management team in a Dialogue Workshop. The Lean Six Sigma program is officially launched and individual targets are established. A training and execution plan is developed and achievement milestones will be used as yardstick to measure the success. A target number of resources to be committed to the program are finalized.

The management also conducts a workshop for project selection and identification. The basis of this workshop can be from the annual review of customer's satisfaction survey or employee's opinion survey or even the management's strategy for aggressive growth and expansion. The Management can also consider using mid to long term planning tools such as the Multi-Generation Planning to set metrics and measure achievement.

The projects identified are documented as project charters. Resources would be assigned to execute the project, initially as Lean Six Sigma training projects. The projects would be evaluated based on a benefit and effort criteria and prioritised for launch. It would be scheduled to coincide with the start of the Green Belt, Black Belt or Lean training.

NURTURE Phase: The change agents are trained and a project selection process is established and put to practice. DMAIC is made into the methodology for continuous improvement.

In this phase, the change agents would undergo the prerequisite leadership and Lean Six Sigma training. They would then undertake training projects that reflect improvements required by their customers in terms of quality, costs and speed. Occasionally, the change agents would be assigned with projects to improve their own area of work or process within the organization.

> "When you're finished changing,
> you're finished."
> *– Benjamin Franklin*

In addition to the training, the change agents are also coached individually on practical application of the toolsets and adherence to the DMAIC cycle. A knowledge transfer process from the consultant teams (typically known as the Master Black Belts) and the trainee change agents takes place during this phase.

The deployment by and large is monitored by the deployment champion to ensure that the projects adhere to the DMAIC cycle. Gate reviews are conducted at the respective DMAIC phase and is attended by stakeholders, sponsors and process owners. The Master Black Belt would be responsible in coaching the management team on monitoring the key milestones and expected outcomes of each DMAIC phase.

The progress of continuous improvement projects is made visible and shared throughout the organization. The management would review the overall progress of all projects every quarter year and remove barriers that deter the advancement of projects within the DMAIC phases.

	Generation 1 - Stop The Bleeding	Generation 2 - Healing the Wound	Generation 3 - Making a Facelift
Key Activities	Develop The Baseline	Expand Knowledge	Engage Customers
	Use DMAIC	Apply Best Practices	Unified Strategy and Execution
	Identify Initiatives	Maintain Consistency	Aligned Success
Generate Output	Monitor Results	Projects Across Businesses	Improved VOC
	Benchmark	Uniformity of DMAIC	Concerted Improvements
Tools & Platform	DMAIC, VSM	DMAIC, RACI	Communication Tools
	Time & Value Analysis	Communication Plans	RACI, Stakeholder Management
	FMEA, Root Cause	Workshops Gate Review	Satisfaction Surveys, Kano Model

Figure 9.2 : Multi Generation Plan

RAISE Phase: Lean Six Sigma toolsets are mastered. The success of projects using the toolsets are shared, leveraged and publicised throughout the organization. Knowledge transfer is enabled.

Projects and resources are identified across the organization at a wider scale. Geographical boundaries are eliminated and targets are set for all segments of businesses and departments.

Project selection workshops are conducted annually and reviewed half yearly. Projects are filled in a pipeline, prioritised and launched when resources become available. The alignment to strategy and goal is maintained throughout the course of activities. Success would be measured against the initial metrics that were set to measure achievement.

A new wave of change agents are identified and trained to maintain the momentum of change and continuous improvement. Coaching of new Black Belts and Green Belts are led by experienced internal Black Belts. Creativity and customised approaches that produced the best results are shared and made into best practices. The roles of Champions, Sponsors, change agents and the workforce play become the cornerstone of a sustainability structure.

Role	Responsibilities
Responsible	• Ensure the job / initiative gets done; can be shared responsibility • Communicate upward (accountable role) • Proactive in driving initiatives
Accountable	• Overall responsible - - "The Buck Stops Here" • Appropriately Senior Role within Country • Own initiative outputs and overall authority to accept outputs
Consulted	• Within the loop of communication • Participate in priority settings
Informed	• Communication and guidance

Figure 9.3 : Sustainability Structure

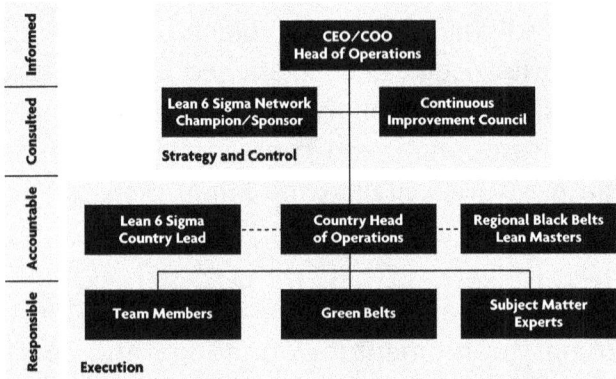

Figure 9.4 : Roles & Responsibility for Sustainability

IMPLANT Phase: Toolsets and the methodology are part of business routine. It is no longer an effort. Change is now a proactive endeavour.

DMAIC tools are utilised in every reporting document and meeting, both internal and external. Solutions to continuous efforts are aligned to the Lean Six Sigma toolsets and DMAIC methodology. The growth of knowledge and the mastery of toolsets and methodology become mature.

The external consulting team begins to play the role of quality and capability assessor. The dependency on external support for training application of toolsets is gradually reduced. Eventually, the need for external support would diminish.

This is the phase where Lean Six Sigma becomes fully institutionalised. The philosophy of change is embraced in its totality by the organization and is demonstrated through actions and examples. The encoding of the organization's DNA takes effect.

Conclusion

Every organization will have and should have its own sustainability process. The process shown here has worked for the financial services organization. Nevertheless, the conceptual visualization can differ between industries and businesses. The end goal remains the same, change is no longer an effort.

Tool- Tips, Case Study, Newsletters

Movers & Shakers Award

Lean 6 Sigma Network & Council

Lean 6 Sigma Champion

Knowledge Transfer

Library & Best Practice Share-point

Training & Coaching

Branding & Marketing

Financial Rewards

Chapter 10
Commencing Thoughts

Fundamental
– serving as a basis supporting existence.
Webster's Online Dictionary

When businesses "tighten the belt" it often means that they have begun to focus on cost savings to brace the impact of reducing revenue. The global economic forecast for the year 2009 and 2010 is bleak. The pressure is on for all businesses worldwide and challenging times are on the horizon. Businesses need to consider returning to the fundamentals.

Contrary to traditional cost saving measures, everyone within an organization needs to know and understand the answers to three fundamental questions:
- Why does the business exist?
- What value proposition is being delivered to the customers?
- How can it effectively meet customer needs?

Returning to the fundamentals begins with improving operational efficiency and effectively optimizing processes to ensure that value is always delivered to the customers.

This requires business leaders in organizations to recommence change and practice to adopt the changes. Change commences with a continuous improvement and innovation culture that follows:-

- an essential thorough review of improvement ideas;
- incorporating into the business operating agenda an optimisation of product creation and service delivery processes; and
- establishing a goal to reduce wasteful processes and process steps.

Continuous improvement activities give rise to the ability to innovate best practices, maximize value add and establish the operational foundation that is needed to meet the customer's need.

In the coming years, businesses need to develop the ability to change, adapt and respond even faster to customers. Businesses need the ability to rapidly produce and deliver value that originates from knowing and understanding a customers' "desire" to meeting a customers "need".

It is the combination of continuous improvement and innovation, today, which would position the business to remain "fresh" and enable it to take advantage when better times come around in the future.

"Changing with Lean Six Sigma
is the beginning of a wonderful and
fulfilling journey for any business.
The knowledge gained during this journey
is for all to share and experience.
The results, the financial gains
– is what you own!"
– A. Aruleswaran

lean6 sigma

LSS Academy Sdn Bhd, an MSC Status Company, is a thought leader and a Center of Excellence in applying and deploying Lean Six Sigma to manufacturing and service based industries in the Asia Pacific Region. LSS Academy's deep, value-based management expertise provides a clear framework to connect value creation priorities to Lean Six Sigma project planning and execution initiatives. This enables maximizing value and return of investment to the shareholder.

Founded in 2007, it aims to create foundations in capability, technology and cultural change management to accomplish, achieve and sustain greater returns of shareholder value. LSS Academy is creating a record of successful implementation of Lean Six Sigma whilst building the thought-leading practices in the critical areas of value creation.

LSS Academy delivers the strategic insight and execution methodology that is required to surpass the goals of growth, speed and cost to businesses, organizations and the personnel that are driving towards continuous improvement, innovations and complexity elimination.

LSS Academy's unique value creation approach is to build business cultures by addressing all four leadership levels: personal, interpersonal, managerial and organisational – that creates a sustainability effect on the capability to grow and succeed in a changing environment.

http://www.lss-academy.com